Oy Vey,

KRISSEL

Printed in the United States of America
ISBN 978-1-54396-256-7

Edited by Lorna Owen
Information regarding Jewish immigration to the United States,
Wikipedia, The Free Encyclopedia

This book reflects the author's present recollections of experiences over time. Names of individuals have been changed to respect their and their descendants' privacy.

For my mother

CONTENTS

CONTENTS

PREFACE

About eight years ago, inspired by old home movies that I had come across, I decided I would jot down some things about my family—many of whom had already passed away—and my childhood, and try to capture not only the times but also the emotions I had in my youth. After writing a few pages, I could see that the transformative moment in my life had been the change from a childhood spent in a primarily Jewish school and Jewish camps to teenage years and beyond in what were then considered Waspy girls high schools and colleges, and in my marriage to "Superwasp."

I could also see that my mother, Kitty, was indeed the dominant person in my childhood. I began to realize that she was fairly typical of her generation of Jewish wives and mothers

1

who were fortunate to have been raised with a great amount of economic comfort. And as I continued to write, it occurred to me that the way she and her family and friends—whom I would come to know as "The Gang"—had lived was unique to the times; it was a rarified environment—and one that I was happy to share.

But, in truth, since Mom was still alive and might not have appreciated the stories I sought to tell, I put the pages in a drawer and forgot about them until I met a publisher and author, Richard Mason, at a cocktail party. After a few drinks, I told him about my tentative steps to writing a book, and to my surprise and dismay, he insisted on seeing the few brief chapters I had written in their raw, unedited form. Wonder of wonders, he liked what he saw and encouraged me to continue working on this book. (Thank you, Richard, for your support!)

As I reached the penultimate chapter, "Missing Kitty (about my mother)," I started to cry. Memories don't just exist in the brain; they live in the body. And memories of all the people from my childhood, who no longer are alive, flooded my heart, making me even more aware of what our lives mean and how very short they are.

For the children who are now elderly, who grew up as part of this generation of Jewish families, I hope the book will bring back memories of their own childhoods. For people who had no exposure to this generation of upper middle class Jewish families, I hope that they will welcome learning about the culture.

I have tried to make this book a humorous one. Making fun of things has always gotten me through the hard and hurtful times, and this book is no exception.

ROLL CAMERA

Home movies, found in the attic of one of my cousins, presently claim my attention for hours on end. I can't understand what happened to this family. The films, which are mostly shot at my grandfather Morris's huge weekend place in Mount Kisco, New York, show everyone in a state of great happiness: swimming in the pool, ice skating on the frozen pond, playing tennis on the property's court, and golfing on its four-hole golf course. Even my formidable grandfather appears easygoing; he is laughing as he pushes us grandchildren on sleds down the snowy hill and takes us "hunting" through the woods, instructing us how to point our fake guns at imagined enemies—most probably Nazis.

In my memory, however, Morris had been a domineering figure, always ordering everyone around. As I grew older, he insisted on my brother, John, and me being formally presented to him and our grandmother, Esther, every Sunday afternoon before the serving of tea and cookies—as if Morris was trying to imitate an English aristocratic lifestyle found in some book or movie.

As the film reel advances, I see my cousin, Peter, and me on the swing, in the hammock, and dangerously racing down a hill on our bicycles. We are holding hands and constantly kissing each other. In fact, those movies show it was a total kiss fest with this family—everyone smacking everyone else on the cheeks or the lips. I am shocked to see my Aunt Mimi and Peter repeatedly kissing on the lips. Was that normal or healthy? Mother and son? And there I am in the pool with my darling father, Irving, and sitting on the lap of Uncle Roger (Mimi's husband and Peter's father), who paid a lot of attention to me since I was the only girl in the family of my generation.

Wonderful birthday parties took place in Mount Kisco, and now I appear on-screen in an exquisite dress from Martha's exclusive Park Avenue boutique, cutting my cake and seemingly ecstatic with the whole show. My beloved governess is flitting around making sure all my wants are fulfilled. Aunt Mimi is batting her eyelashes and looking beautiful. Kitty is cute and flirtatious and smiling—which seems at odds with the mother I remember. The Gang is sitting around the pool eating a gorgeous lunch and hamming it up for the camera…

I search these movies to try to find clues—any clues at all that might reveal what lay in store for this deliriously happy family.

IN THE BEGINNING

They came to America fleeing vicious anti-Semitism, pogroms, government restrictions, and poverty. They came from Russia, and from Central and Eastern Europe—between 1880 and 1924, the latter in numbers of over two million. They were very poor merchants, shopkeepers and craftsmen. They were seeking freedom to practice their religion and opportunities to educate their children and start their own businesses.

It was in that large wave of Eastern European immigrants that my grandfather, Morris, came to the US and set up home on New York City's Lower East Side. That's about all I know of his early years. He was typical of so many Jewish immigrants who put their personal histories behind them as soon as they reached America's shores, rarely discussing their childhoods in far-off lands. He said very little about his relatives. What he did talk about were his first jobs: selling newspapers as a kid in New York and being a messenger boy for a company that made brown grocery bags.

He later became a super-salesman for that same company and was then hired by Hudson Pulp and Paper, which was owned by three prominent Jewish families. Apparently one of the owners fought with the other two and left the company, taking the Equitable Paper Bag Division and Morris with him. Morris was quickly made Sales Manager of Equitable, and eventually an equal partner. In the end, Morris got rid of his partner and became the sole proprietor of Equitable.

By 1941, the year I came into the world, Morris's Equitable Paper Bag Company had become a prosperous business, which provided a comfortable upper middle class lifestyle for him and his family—his wife and daughters, Kitty and Mimi; and two sons-in-law, Irving and Roger.

Like other upwardly social and economic mobile Jewish immigrant families who expected the sons to join the family businesses (that were as varied as light socket manufacturers, department and grocery stores, insurance companies, law and real estate firms), Morris—having no sons—demanded that his sons-in-law join his paper bag company. And that is precisely what Irving and Roger did in order to assure him that they could take care of his daughters.

To understand my family you have to understand my grandfather. Everyone who knew him—friends, family members, and even business competitors—agreed that Morris was a genius. He was always working—even when he wasn't in the office. I can still see his note pads and red pencils lying all over the place: by the side of his bed in his Manhattan apartment, on his desk in the library of his country home in Mount Kisco [Westchester County], and later, in his winter residence, nicknamed the "Winter White House," in Palm Beach, Florida— where he would make at least a dozen calls a day to the Equitable offices.

He married my grandmother when she was sixteen years old. From the few pictures I have of Esther as a young woman, she was lovely, always elegantly dressed, wearing pearls and white gloves. But, even in these pictures, standing side-by-side with a short-but-handsome Morris, she seems to be totally dominated by him.

My grandparents' relationship was an open book. Morris would scream "Esther" and she would come running from another room to fetch his slippers (literally) or perform some other subservient task. My entire family, except for me, seemed to think that this was okay and the way things should be—the patriarchs of these Jewish families ruling the roost and ordering everyone around; that was both expected and accepted. The rumor in our family was that Esther had once tried to run away; but sadly without an education—having never finished high school—and no money to speak of, she was "stuck."

A tyrannical figure, Morris continued to wield his authority through his control of the money. I found him rather intimidating and used to be very nervous before going to his apartment to see him since I was never sure what kind of mood he was in, or whether or not he was being nice to Esther. But what helped me to overcome my trepidation was the possibility of getting a peek at his money closet, which never ceased to amaze me. My grandfather would be in his office, and after I paid my respects, he would sometimes go over and open the closet with a key and take out stacks of crisp, fresh bills to give to me. I was convinced he was making that money with a machine hidden in the closet—even though no store manager ever yelled that the money was fake when I spent it. Later, to my great disappointment but also relief, I found out that Morris had got the money in a much less dramatic way; he simply sent someone to the bank with the order that they were to come back with only new, barely touched-by-human-hands bills.

The money closet was also the source of the cash that Morris would hand out all over town—he was an incredible tipper. He would dispense $20 bills as if they were Pez. I remember hundreds of instances of him sliding several bills into an eager paw in order to get the best table in a restaurant. In fact, in one particularly popular restaurant in New York, Morris had the A table near the window and by passing $100 to the maître d', he was guaranteed that he could sit there for as long as he wanted to. (Kitty definitely inherited her father's tipping gene. She would always remind Irving to tip the bellboys, porters, and waiters, and check his hand to make sure he was giving enough).

My grandfather was also a perfectionist (another trait that he passed to Kitty…and me). This was seen most clearly at his country house in Mount Kisco, where even the chicken coop was beautifully constructed and painted; the rocks in the rock garden were kept very clean; and twenty of the forty acres on the estate were mowed and weeded. To this day, I can vividly recall Morris tramping around the land with his weeder in his hand, searching for any tiny weeds that had been missed by the many gardeners.

BROOKLYN

Morris and Esther raised Kitty and Mimi—the girls—in Brooklyn in the Turner Towers apartment house on Eastern Parkway; this was considered one of the most fashionable addresses in Brooklyn. The girls attended and graduated from Erasmus Hall; they went on to marry and start their own families all the while staying within a few feet of each other in the Turner Towers. The three families were perfectly happy living there—but it was still Brooklyn, not Manhattan.

Morris and Esther could never have foreseen what Brooklyn is today—not only a trendy place to live, but also a showcase for prime real estate. Through the decades of the twentieth century the ethnic composition of Brooklyn, with its different neighborhoods, fluctuated constantly as one group of people moved out and another moved in. For example, Brooklyn's Brownsville section had been predominantly Jewish until the 1970s when many of the families left, and then it became mostly African American; and Midwood, where my grandparents once lived, went from being largely Irish to Jewish to Pakistani—my grandparents would have been horrified.

But when I was born in 1941, Morris and Esther were already appalled at the thought that their "little princess" should have to spend even one night in Flatbush. So I was immediately whisked from Doctors Hospital, on the Upper East Side, to the beautiful estate in Mount Kisco, which Morris had recently bought for all three families.

Brooklyn would have never been mentioned again if it weren't for a couple of reasons that kept pulling us back there. First, all of Irving's relatives and Kitty's grandmother still lived in Brooklyn so we had to call on them—which always sent Kitty into paroxysms of anxiety. Something in Brooklyn might be catching. So our visits were far and few between even though I loved my Dad's siblings.

Second, and most importantly, our family physician, Dr. Goldstein, practiced in Brooklyn. Now Dr. Goldstein was one of those doctors who were commonly referred to as old timers. He recommended aspirin and bed rest for every single ailment but was a genius at calming down panicky Jewish mothers.

I hated Dr. Goldstein! He had filthy hands, which I never saw him wash, and Band-Aids on almost every finger. He had a distinctive and horrible odor that I could smell whenever he examined me. He had such a thick Brooklyn accent that I needed a translator—yet Kitty seemed to understand him perfectly and worshipped him fervently.

At last, to my relief, with the trip to Brooklyn taking up so much valuable shopping time, and Dr. Goldstein deciding to retire at the age of ninety-five, Kitty and Mimi discovered—to their amazement—that Manhattan had some doctors who knew what they were doing.

I'm glad that Kitty lived to see the resurgence of Brooklyn, if not Flatbush, as a chic and desirable place to live.

THE GANG

Kitty and Irving, along with Mimi and Roger, were part of the Gang—at least that's what they called it. I know the word "gang" tends to conjure up dark streets with knife fights, the Sharks and the Jets, but, for me, "gang" brings to mind memories of my parents and their tight-knit group of Jewish friends who spent their days playing and partying, flirting and futzing around, and occasionally even feuding with one another.

In the forties, the Gang consisted of about twenty couples of approximately the same age. Many of them met traveling in the same circles, same private clubs and same schools; many were newly married, starting families, and launching their careers. Born into privilege, these young men and women, mostly second-generation Americans, were bound together by the histories of their parents and grandparents who had fled Eastern Europe, and by the shadows that the horrors of the Second World War cast on them— not being far enough removed from the Holocaust to feel that their own existence was totally secure.

They did everything together: weekends at their country houses in Westchester County, north of New York City; memberships in the same Westchester country clubs, and in the Harmonie Club in New York, and in Temple Emanu-El—recognized as the most important temple in the city and, probably, in the world.

Their parties were big, glamorous affairs, usually held at the Harmonie Club, while more intimate dinners, followed by rounds of bridge, took place in their apartments. Lunches were often arranged by the wives either in their homes or at the Club, where they would play games of canasta and mahjong, which were all the rage at the time.

The inner circle of the Gang, organized by Kitty and recognized by all the women, consisted of Kitty, Mimi, Dasha and Roz. Kitty and Mimi often extended their routine morning telephone calls to include the other two women who were their closest friends; but as soon as they hung up the phone, the sisters would call each other to say terrible things about them. For example, Kitty and Mimi might make fun of Roz and the clothes she had worn to a party the night before. Or they would savage Dasha for having flirted with one of their husbands. It wasn't nice.

My mother seemed to be the popular one in the Gang, and I think Mimi was only accepted into the group because she was Kitty's sister. Most of the Gang, I'm sure, could see that my aunt was cold and sometimes mean; however no one would have ever dared to say anything negative about her since Kitty clearly worshipped her sister. She thought Mimi, who was two years her junior, was the most beautiful woman in the world. Comments about Mimi, among the Gang members, were the focus of much speculation on my part.

To my recollection the biggest Gang scandal involved Harriet, who was a tiny little sweetheart and whom I loved. Her husband died in his early fifties and she was devastated. Several months after his passing, she went on a cruise and met an Italian singer—an entertainer on the ship. He was good-looking, very young, and had a terrific accent. Harriet fell madly in love and then made the mistake of bringing him to some of the parties of the Gang. Immediately, they labeled him a "gigolo." He was reviled by the entire group of friends—the inner circle in particular. The women started berating Harriet on a daily basis, telling her how humiliating the romance was for her and for all of them. In the end, Harriet gave up her one true love, crying hysterically for weeks. But the Gang was ecstatic and thought they could make it up to her with little gifts: gloves from Martha's and scarves from Hermès.

In contrast to their treatment of Harriet's lover, the Gang members fell all over themselves trying to impress two couples not quite within their grasp. One of the couples came from Cape Town, South Africa, which sounded like a mysterious and glamorous place. And the fact that the husband and wife had British accents set them apart and lent them a movie-star aura.

The other couple owned the leading department store chain in the New York area and was the richest of them all; their apartment was palatial and their country estate was featured in magazines. In Palm Beach, they had one of the mansions on the ocean, admired and coveted by all. Their daughters went to the same all-girls high school that I did. (In fact I think my mother purposefully sent me there since she was determined to give me everything that those kids had; she couldn't get her mind off this family and their great riches and public prominence.) I didn't like the mother. She wasn't always nice to her kids and had an affected accent, which was not normal for Ashkenazi Jews—and I knew it! I wouldn't suck up to her, which upset Kitty greatly, and I couldn't stand it when I'd hear my mother telling her how wonderful she was.

In any case I was expected to treat all the couples in the Gang as family, which was hard because, in addition to the above mother, I found some of the women to be phony and obnoxious. But not Doris. She was my favorite—besides Harriet, of course. Doris was the nicest mother I had ever met. She never nagged her children, never bragged about them or made them perform in front of others. *Was she really Jewish?* I often wondered. Also, I had a big crush on Doris's handsome and aloof son, prompting me to spend as much time at her house as possible.

Given the amount of socializing, we kids—the next generation—essentially grew up together. We attended the same private schools and same summer camps. And on weekends and holidays in the country, we went to each other's houses. That was de rigueur.

Annually, a party at the Country Club included a show-off-your-children talent show. I dreaded those evenings since I would be propped up on the piano stool and forced to play "But Not for Me"—the only piano piece I ever learned and, thus, had to repeat year after year. That little talent show brought out the nastiest competitive feelings in the Gang, even more so than their matches on tennis courts and rounds of golf at the Club. Nevertheless, they would cover up their feelings with effusive comments about the talents of each other's children— but everyone knew what everyone was really thinking.

Then there was the time when I was about four years old. I was at yet another party and the highlight of it was when my little boyfriend and I decided to take down our pants when we were by ourselves at the swimming pool. That was the first time I had ever seen *it*. *It* was a little wobbly thing that made me laugh hysterically. Decades later he became a major financial mogul in New York (despite his mother's frequently voiced opinion that he would never amount to anything), and still to this day when we run into each other at parties, the first thing that pops into my head is the vision of his little tiny *it* and the proud expression on his four-year old face.

The Gang remained steadfast in their loyalty to one another for the rest of their lives—some cut short by illness. I still miss seeing many of them and observing their group chemistry. Their bond was unique. I haven't known any group of people like that since.

DEAR PETER

My cousin Peter was my first love and my first best friend. He was just a year older than I, and we lived together in the same country house in Mount Kisco and the same apartment house on Fifth Avenue until we were out of college. He was very handsome and I was proud to be his cousin and considered him my brother. He was very smart and would eventually graduate from college summa cum laude—although when we were children I had no idea that he was *that* smart.

As a little boy, he was full of fun and, during our time in Mount Kisco, Peter and I spent every waking minute together since we were not allowed to play with the goyim down the road for fear they might be contagious. They were Catholic—a total no-no in Morris's book of acceptable friends.

Morris had purchased the Mount Kisco property before I was born, and moved our three families to live there full-time because he was certain that a bomb was going to fall directly onto Manhattan and the Westchester estate happened to have a bomb shelter—in which we would later stockpile thousands of cans of "delicious" treats like string beans. The property had forty acres with a river running through it, a tennis court, a swimming pool and pool house, a playground with swings and slides, a mini golf course for my father, a pond with a canoe, and a chicken coop with real chickens.

Peter and I adored that place. We spent most of the days sprinting across the property to the waterfall, figuring out how to get away from Sadie, his governess, and sneaking into the kitchen where Julia, the cook, was truly nice to us. We played with our fake guns and shot frogs with bows and arrows. We played with marbles for hours. Peter brought out my most competitive spirit and I spent a lot of my childhood trying to beat him in everything from swimming to jacks.

Sometimes, at night, we were allowed to play with jack knives in front of the back porch or to light incense, which we loved. We would run down to the river and swing for hours on the one swing or lie together in the hammock, making up stories. Our favorite one was how we would run away and go to Paris or some other exotic city where we would live by ourselves in a huge mansion. Although we were very competitive, we were very loyal to each other and would form a team against anyone who tried to interfere in our friendship.

Peter was a normal, mischievous little boy. But when he was thought to have been rude or when he didn't sit up straight at the dinner table, Roger, his father, would take him down to the bomb shelter where he would be spanked. Finally the bomb shelter had a purpose after all. While this was going on, I used to sit on top of the huge TV in the library, sobbing uselessly in front of the rest of the family. Afterward, I would console Peter and implore him to leave his family and join mine.

One afternoon Peter and I finally decided to run away. I remember we packed our little suitcases, made it down the long gravel driveway to the road and went as far as the goyim. Then the idea of crossing in front of the *Catholic* house scared us so much that we immediately turned back home and unpacked our bags. Our governesses had been gossiping in the kitchen about the family, completely unaware of our little adventure, so no one ever knew.

Every Fourth of July Morris would throw a huge party with fireworks. All his celebrity politician pals, whom he cultivated through huge donations, would show up and salivate at the sight of the beautiful, illegal fireworks show. Since Thomas Dewey, the Governor of New York, always came to the party, I would be presented to him in my very best summer dress. One year he took me into the woods with his security guards and taught me how to shoot a real gun. The toy guns I played with—that, for me, were like the guns in the comic books we devoured—could never compare with the real thing. I was in heaven and worshipped Governor Dewey forever.

The years with Peter in Mount Kisco were idyllic. But when it was time for Peter and me to begin school, our families moved back to New York City and Mount Kisco became our weekend home. That is when Peter started to change; eventually he became a troubled teenager. We didn't go to the same school so I couldn't watch over him during the day—still, he was like the other half of me and I could sense how miserable he was. He seemed to do well enough with his classes but, during those years, he couldn't get along at all with Mimi and Roger and they made no attempt, as far as I could see, to understand what was troubling him. Those weren't the days of child psychiatry, so a kid was either good or bad—and they labeled Peter bad. Mimi poured her affection onto Stevie, his little brother, and Bambi, the ridiculous little dog to which she was devoted. In fact, I would venture that Bambi was the real love of her life. She would talk about her dog constantly and smother him with the kisses that had once been reserved for Peter.

Since he tested so well and had pretty good marks, Peter got into Duke and seemed to get through freshman year without any major problems. But during his sophomore year he started to get into real trouble and was found with a prostitute in his room—which was grounds for dismissal. These days you can keep anything you want in a college room, but that was a different era. I was at Smith College when Peter got kicked out and he came up to see me for a few days, but I knew I was losing him. He didn't really confide in me any longer and I felt heartsick and helpless.

When I watch the home movies of when we were little, the two of us so happy and having so much fun together, it is almost impossible to fathom what happened to Peter—although I still hold Mimi and Roger responsible.

From Duke, Peter went on to Boston University where he succeeded brilliantly (academically) and seemed to be fairly stable emotionally. Soon after graduation he went to work for Equitable, got married, had three children, and moved out of New York City. The gulf between us became unbridgeable. I heard through the family grapevine that things had gotten worse for him; his marriage was apparently on the rocks and he wanted a divorce. Then his wife suddenly died in the bathtub from (according to Mimi) an aneurysm, so he didn't need the divorce after all. To the family's relief he met another woman whom he married and had a child with—Peter's fourth.

Just when I was hoping things were finally turning around for him, Peter abruptly died. I had come back from a business trip when my husband told me that my cousin had drowned in Barbados. There were a few different stories about how it happened. The family version—and the one I prefer—was that while the new wife and baby were lying on the beach, he had gone swimming with his three older children in an area where swimming was prohibited, but he didn't care. That was Peter. He then went back to join his young family when he heard his kids start to scream. They were drowning out by a coral reef. Peter immediately leapt back into the water and managed to pull all three of them up onto the reef—right before he himself went down in a whirlpool. So, although he shouldn't have been swimming in the dangerous waters in the first place, he was a hero in the end—and I like to think of him that way. The hero from my childhood, who died saving his children.

I think about Peter all the time. *What if he had lived? Would we have become best friends again as our families got older? Would I have been able to help him with his problems if we had become as close as we were when we were kids?* I will never know any of this and it makes me very sad. It is one thing in my life that I am unable to handle with humor.

"DOESN'T EVERYONE?"

Not until I was about six years old did I know that not everyone lived in hotels.

The Dorset Hotel, to which we moved when I was five years old, was located on West 54th Street between 5th and 6th Avenues. It was built in 1926 by the architect Emery Roth and was both a regular hotel and an apartment hotel. Our family had three apartments there—presumably bought by Morris: one for my grandparents, one for our family, and one for Mimi's family.

This replication of our living situation at the Turner Towers in Brooklyn and our house in Mount Kisco was an extreme situation that most of the other families in the Gang did not follow. The fact that each family had its own apartment was just a minor detail. It was the feeling of all of us being together in case of an emergency that mattered. It was also Morris's way of keeping the entire family under his control. The funny thing is, there wasn't a lot of dropping in or, even, formal visits. Instead there was a hot telephone network that would exhaust even a modern day AT&T.

Like Eloise at the Plaza, I had the run of the Dorset, and the doormen and elevator men treated me like the little princess I was supposed to be. In fact, *The Little Princess* was my favorite book, and I spent hours listening to my governess, Fraulein, read about the dark attic where the rich little heroine was banished after her father was presumably killed. It was so easy to imagine myself sent to the attic of the Dorset where I would sleep on the floor without any heat and would be friendly with the rats and roaches until a distinguished old gentleman saved me, and made me rich again.

Down the hall from our apartment lived my parents' best friends, the Rosensteins. Their daughter, Ruthie, was in love with my brother and spent most of her free time chasing him around the hallways, trying to grab his identification bracelet. In those days, wearing someone's identification bracelet meant you were going steady. John didn't like Ruthie and a battle ensued. The families got involved. Some kind of compromise was worked out whereby Ruthie got the bracelet and then returned it, thus allowing her to save face and our mothers to remain friends.

While Ruthie was making my brother miserable I was being made miserable as well by the food at the Dorset. Kitty would order from room service three times a day and the meals were, in fact, some form of torture. I grew to hate the starving Armenians about whom Kitty constantly reminded me as I stared down at the overcooked broccoli or carrots or spinach that were placed in front of my nose. I would sit at the dining room table, my eyes glued on the mushy vegetables, refusing to eat them. My parents and brother would leave to do other things, only to return hours later to find me still poised above my plate.

The only respite from those horrible meals was dinner on Sunday nights, when we, like most New York Jewish families, went for Chinese food. Ruby Foo's on the Upper West Side was Kitty and Irving's restaurant of choice, and I would always order chow mein. But Sunday to the next Sunday was a long time to wait. To tide me over, I would sneak off to the hotel's kitchen whenever Fraulein was napping. I became a real hit with the staff who loved to fill me with juicy morsels of cheesecake and chocolate chip cookies that Kitty was afraid would make me fat.

DARLING FRAULEIN

Wealthy young people and working Moms today have nannies. But in my childhood they were called governesses and most of them were German refugees who got out of Germany before Hitler came to power or in the early part of his regime.

While Sadie was the governess for my cousins, Fraulein was the governess for me and my brother—although I chose to ignore that arrangement since I wanted her completely to myself. Sadie and Fraulein seemed to get along okay, but I don't think Fraulein trusted her. Unlike Fraulein who was German, Sadie was Canadian, which was highly unusual—but which Mimi loved because it set her governess apart—and, to Mimi, that meant hers was better. Sadie was tough though. She was nice enough to me, but very protective of Peter, and she hated it when I would steal his trucks and toy guns and replace them with my dolls. Her face would register the meanest look possible and she would hiss her disapproval.

Fraulein was another story. She came to us via a German employment agency to take care of my brother John when he was a toddler; then she took care of me when I was born. She was very pretty with blue eyes and beautiful creamy skin. Her pale blond hair was very long, and she wound it around her head in braids. She was the sweetest person in the world and she was my world. She did all the diaper changes and baths, and wrapped her arms around me when I was disappointed or distressed. She sang me German lullabies. She was still bathing me when I was ten years old—why not?! In Mount Kisco, Fraulein and I slept in the same room and I still remember waking up and watching her move around the room, which made me feel very secure and happy. And she always called me "darling"—no matter what. In her opinion, I had a permanent halo around my head, the head of her angel.

Even my toilet training became an occasion to celebrate with Fraulein. It took hours. (But, look at it this way, what would have happened if it hadn't worked!) The toilet training started with my mother, who had probably heard somewhere that she was supposed to do it. She placed me on the small potty and stood there impatiently waiting for something to happen. Tenacity has always been one of my strongest virtues, especially in the face of adversity—even at this early age. So I sat there until, finally, Kitty erupted into a frenzy of frustrated emotions. "For God's sake," she screamed, her hands flying around her shoulders, "Just do it and get it over with"; she wanted to get back to the telephone.

Passively, I remained on my tiny throne, wide-eyed and innocent, but nary a tinkle emerged from my little body. After a few hours she gave up, and my beloved Fraulein walked into the perfectly decorated pink and white country bathroom.

"Toni darling, what's the matter honey? Do a little wee-wee for Fraulein, please sweetheart." And within seconds, we had a veritable waterfall.

Fraulein's relationship with Kitty was periodically tense especially when Kitty spied me wrapping my arms around her and telling her how much I loved her. What did Kitty expect? She hadn't done the dirty work and she wasn't my sweet Fraulein.

Fraulein had a husband whose name was Odd, which I thought was very strange. He was Swedish and had been a sailor in the navy. Once in a while Fraulein would take me to her small apartment in Flushing where I would be made to feel like a queen on a visit to her subjects. Fraulein would serve me a glorious meal of stuff I liked, like hot dogs, and Odd would tell me tales of his life in the navy while Fraulein would smile at him, full of love. I loved it there and dreamed of moving in with Fraulein and Odd forever. I could sleep in the kitchen—I wouldn't care.

When I was eleven years old Kitty broke the terrible news: Fraulein was no longer going to be my full-time governess. Instead, she would babysit from time to time, especially on the weekends. The news left me in despair. Every week I hoped and prayed that Irving would take Kitty with him to the Club both Saturday and Sunday so I could be left alone with my beloved Fraulein.

In addition to all her other wonderful attributes, she loved Blueboy, my parakeet, as much as I did, and when I went away to college, she took him to her home where he lived out the rest of his life. I couldn't wait for vacations, when I would get to see her. I continued to adore Fraulein and called her as often as possible. After I got married, she came to my apartment every Christmas so my kids got to know her.

But Fraulein got frailer and frailer. She was just a little thing anyway, but she began to resemble a tiny little bird and I was afraid her bones would break. She ate practically nothing and, although I sent her money once in a while, I learned later that she was on food stamps since Kitty didn't send her anything. I began to lose contact with her as she became increasingly weaker and I talked, instead, to her nephew who had moved into her apartment after Odd died in his eighties. I got more and more worried because her nephew didn't sound very stable and Fraulein was often too tired to come to the phone. Finally, when she turned ninety, I insisted on coming out to Flushing to see her and what I saw was appalling. The apartment was filthy; there was food everywhere and it didn't look as if any-one had picked up or cleaned in months. The windows were so dirty you couldn't see out of them. Fraulein was so weak I was afraid she was going to die right in front of me. I felt sick to my stomach.

I wanted to bring Fraulein home to live with me, but that would have been rough on my family, so I hired a service to clean her place once a week, and the Visiting Nurse Service to stop in on a regular basis to make sure that she was okay and that her nephew was taking proper care of her. She died not many years afterward, but at least I knew that in her final days she had been provided for and kept safe.

I will always miss my Fraulein. Her whole life was devoted to my happiness. Bless you, Fraulein, and may you be in heaven, watching over my family with Blueboy on your shoulder.

BLUEBOY

Everyone has a way of dealing with family relations throughout their childhood. For some, it is remaining as silent and invisible as possible at all times of the day, carrying a book everywhere to hide behind. For others, it is pretending that school and other assorted activities are stages for their outstanding talents so there can be nothing but praise at home. And still for others, it is lying about their activities outside of the home so as not to be interrogated; or throwing themselves into sports so they are away from home as much as possible. But for me, it took the form of a bird.

On my tenth birthday my grandmother, Esther, gave me a blue parakeet that I promptly adored and called Blueboy. My mother was not a fan of this gift and tried to get rid of him, but I became hysterical at the thought and promised to assume total responsibility for him and clean the poo-poos out of his cage.

Eventually, I realized that Blueboy was my secret weapon: a way to keep Kitty out of my room most of the day and ensure my privacy. To that end, I would let him out of his cage where he would fly madly around the room until he settled on my shoulder or my head, nuzzling me with his little beak and depositing poo-poos on me or on the furniture, where he also loved to land. So, before Kitty even dared to come into my room, she would yell out, asking if Blueboy was in his cage, and I would happily yell back, no, he wasn't.

Parakeets are very smart and learn how to talk. I began spending hours with Blueboy teaching him words and phrases in English and French and giving him little treats when he repeated them. The amazing thing was that he learned just when to say the right thing to me. Whenever I would have a bad day at school, I'd open his cage and he would settle on my shoulder and say, "Don't cry, sweetheart, Blueboy loves you."

One day Kitty came roaring into my room to nag me about something or other and Blueboy began running around his cage. "Here comes that bitch!" he screamed loudly. "What, what did that bird say?" my mother demanded, her eyes wide with amazement and Blueboy-hatred. I immediately answered that it wasn't anything that we could understand.

Thus began a war between Blueboy and Kitty that, over time, got uglier and uglier. First she insisted, unsuccessfully, on giving him to a friend or to someone else in the family, preferably her sister Mimi—who I did think could use a few direct words from a parakeet. Then one afternoon, when I came home early from school, I found Kitty standing at my bedroom window with Blueboy's cage in her hands. The window was open and the cage door was open, but smart old Blueboy wasn't going anywhere. In fact, a chorus of "No, no, never, never" emphatically emanated from the cage until I ran over to him and saved his life. Kitty knew she had been defeated.

Blueboy continued to help me get through my teenage years until I left for college and Fraulein took him and gave him all her love and care.

NEAT AND CLEAN

The relationships of Jewish women with their German maids in the mid-1900s have always fascinated me. Was this a way of getting back at Germany for the ovens? The obsession of the Jewish housewife with the German maid, however, was a phenomenon of the times. Later on, our aging mothers would instead hire illegal Filipino and Brazilian women to work for them.

My mother's relationship with her cleaning maids was always quite extraordinary. It would not be an exaggeration to say that her household staff were the most important people in her life. She hated them; she loved them; and, as for the cleaning ladies, she was not only obsessed with their skills but also with their conduct and personal habits. If, by accident, one of them put her hands on the walls or had messy hair, she would be subjected to a distressing flow of criticism from Kitty. I rarely heard my mother discuss her friends in the same amount of detail with which she used to describe her maids.

Kitty also had a love-hate relationship with Fraulein. She was totally dependent on her, but she wasn't always nice to her; she loved the power that came from treating Fraulein as an indentured servant. On the other hand, Kitty let Katie the Cook take total control; my mother never made any decisions without first consulting Katie.

Katie the Cook started working for us when I was eleven years old, after we moved to Fifth Avenue, and she became the absolute ruler of our household. I always thought she was the domineering husband my mother secretly longed for. And I hated Katie the Cook.

She was stocky and humorless and I lived in fear of Fraulein's days off, knowing that Katie would take over. She simply wasn't nice and she certainly wasn't pretty. In fact, I didn't even like most of the food she made, which was dry and overcooked. But, according to my mother, Katie was *it* in our household. If, for example, Kitty wanted to give a party, it would be up to Katie to say yes or no, and even whether or not my grandmother should be invited. Also, Katie did not believe in breaking the rules. If you were more than thirty seconds late to dinner there would be hell to pay, and Katie would dispense the cold and silent treatment for weeks.

Katie the Cook lasted for decades. Then her husband decided they should go back to Germany and my mother was cut asunder. After Katie left, twenty cooks followed her in quick succession as none of them ever measured up: this one forgot to wipe out the sink after dinner; that one forgot to take off her shoes upon entering the apartment; and the rest of them were "stupid, stupid, stupid," or, more pointedly, "*draikops*."

The year my mother died, I remember her talking on the phone ecstatically about her very last maid. "Well anyway, she's a wonderful, fabulous cleaner. She climbs the walls and takes down the curtains. She cleans out the closets and wipes down all the books. I love her!" These were the things that mattered to Kitty. At least she died happy in the knowledge that a wonderful maid would take care of cleaning and distributing all the household goods.

"I WANNA GO BACK TO TRIPP LAKE CAMP"

When Irving, an extraordinary athlete, came home from work he liked to stand upside down on one finger and hop around on it much to my amazement and joy and Kitty's distress. So it is no surprise that he was keen for his children to love sports as much as he did; he threw me in the swimming pool when I was two years old and I had to learn to swim. That was just the beginning. I loved sports from that age on and always wanted to make him proud of my athletic achievements. In elementary school, I played on the boys' baseball team, and at Vega, my first camp, I won the tennis tournament when I was eight years old. But it was at Tripp Lake Camp in Maine where I began to succeed in many sports, winning "best all-around athlete" trophies and becoming number one in tennis and swimming. At the end of each summer, I would descend from the camp train with an armful of trophies, which delighted Irving—and that made me happy.

How did my mother take all of this? She had no affinity for sports—as a participant or as a spectator. Maybe she could have been a good athlete if she had tried—although shopping is extremely aerobic and that might have counted. In any case Kitty didn't relate to my love of sports and rarely came to watch me, but she showed her appreciation in her own way. For example, she had replicas made of all my trophies (since I had to return the real ones to the camp the following summer—that was the rule). And because of her unexpected thoughtfulness I'm still able to gaze at my trophies and remember my days of glory…while I rub my lower back.

Tripp Lake Camp was and is a Jewish girls camp and, during my time, a very competitive, athletic one. When I was ten years old I had to be interviewed by the owners, Miss Kitty and Aunt Caroline—two classy Jewish ladies from Philadelphia, before I was accepted; they made a big deal of how many great athletes went to the camp—at which point I vowed to win all their athletic trophies and become the best Tripp Lake camper ever.

Aunt Caroline was the tough businesswoman and the disciplinarian—in other words the bad guy. Miss Kitty was the roly-poly sweetheart whom all the campers went to with their problems and who was everyone's ideal granny. The counselors all went to colleges like Sargent or Bouve in Boston where they could pursue majors in physical education.

The worst part of camp—the only part that I hated—were the camping trips. I didn't mind canoeing, but then we had to lift the heavy canoes out of the lake and drag them onto the shore. From there we would continue on to the camping ground where we had to set up heavy tents and help in cooking our own meals—a far cry from our family's kitchen, run by Katie the Cook.

The mountain climbing trips were even worse. I never found that the excitement of reaching the summit and gazing over the land of Maine ever made up for the horrible trek with all the heavy equipment and the bug-filled nights in a claustrophobic tent, lying wide awake. Luckily, none of those trips ever lasted more than a few days and we could get back to our camp and my beloved sports.

The first week of one's last year as a camper—the campers are fifteen years old—four captains and eight managers would be elected. When I realized that was the case, I started doing two things the year before the election. First, knowing that we would choose our teammates if we got elected captains, I started watching the baseball, field hockey and other games of the younger campers to scout out whom I wanted to recruit for my team. Second, I needed votes from the younger campers and so I made the decision, as a result of a brainstorm in the middle of the night, to set up a free hair-cutting salon,

In front of my tent every evening, I posted an irresistible sign about fantastic free haircuts, with sample pictures of glamorous heads from beauty magazines, and managed to procure a pair of not-too-sharp scissors. The first camper came up to the tent and sat down on the chair and I went to work cutting as much hair as possible in a straight line. She thought she looked great so I started getting flooded with requests for haircuts. Campers from age seven to fifteen went to breakfast the next day with the Krissel Cut, which could be paid for with the assurance of voting for me for captain the next summer.

Unfortunately, the frightening Aunt Caroline heard about it and stomped up to the tent in a fury. "What is going on here?" she demanded. When I told her I thought I could help out their mothers by giving the girls haircuts before they went home, her face turned purple and she tore off my sign and took away my scissors. Well, that might have been the end of my haircutting career, but it ensured that I was a captain the next summer. And I didn't stay on the bad side of Aunt Caroline for too long since she loved the good athletes.

I still sing a lot of my camp songs and remember almost all the words. "I Wanna Go Back to Tripp Lake Camp in Dear Old Poland Maine" was, and remains, my favorite. Sometimes I wave my arms around, conducting the songs like I did as a song leader after the song leader on my team had a nervous breakdown because she was so bad in sports and didn't belong at Tripp Lake Camp.

Best years of my life? Maybe!

THE NAZIS ARE COMING TO GET ME

Growing up I found ideas of prison and poverty terrifying—maybe that was provoked by Charles Dickens's tales, or, closer to home, picturing Peter down in the bomb shelter. Nevertheless, it was the Holocaust that flooded me with the most disturbing visions. I often imagined what it would have been like in Dachau or Auschwitz, or what it would have been like to be Anne Frank. And when I let my imagination go wild, I would even envision ovens down the middle of Park Avenue awaiting Jews whom a current Gestapo had driven out of their gorgeous apartments.

In retrospect, I think my fears of the Holocaust must have been nothing compared to those of the older generation who had lived through World War II, which resulted in their isolating themselves among their own "people"—often according to socio-economic class. Jewish country clubs, schools and camps—although often established because Jews were not allowed into Gentile establishments—were seen as safe havens and protected environments. As such, my entire childhood was spent in the company of only Jewish people and kids… that is until my mother had other ideas.

When I was ready to enter ninth grade, Kitty decided to send me to a primarily Gentile private all-girls high school in New York City. I think she honestly thought that this traditional girls school was much better than the liberal, progressive, almost totally Jewish school that I had been attending.

But I was devastated; I didn't want to change schools. Blueboy and I had many conversations about this—and a few more mean words were added to his vocabulary!

* * *

The first day in my new school was a nightmare. First of all, there were no boys! And we were required to wear blue uniforms with white or blue shirts and blue panties. I think if I'd worn make up I would have been thrown out as soon as I entered. Many of my classmates were [gasp] blond with perfectly-shaped, tiny noses that tilted up instead of down. In my class at my old school there was only one blond girl shiksa whose name was Christine—who knew where she had come from? She was the object of much wonderment and most of the boys were in love with her.

Since there was no school bus for my new school, and Kitty was afraid of public transportation, Morris sent me to school every morning in his gorgeous, super-big Cadillac with Henri, the chauffeur, at the wheel. That was so mortifying and so different from how the other kids got to school—even the Rockefellers—that I bribed Henri with candy and made him drop me off three blocks before the school's entrance. This saved me a lot of embarrassment and was kept a deep, dark secret during my high school years.

Weekend house parties with my friends in the new school were frightening. Aristocratic, white-haired mothers established the rules that we had to follow. They certainly never called me *bubelah*, or sweetheart, the names I was used to hearing from the mothers of my Jewish friends. On Sundays we all went to church. Having never been in a church before I was taken aback by the huge gold crosses, always with the same guy with bleeding hands. Why would you go to a church to see this and be depressed? One Sunday the minister said something about Jews that I didn't hear very well, but I remember my friends looking at me weirdly so I knew it must have been something bad.

The very worst parts of those weekends were the hiking trips through the woods, which brought back memories of those at Tripp Lake Camp. I was sure there were fanged animals and snakes behind every tree. Bugs swarmed around our heads, biting at every chance, making hot tears well up in my eyes and my stomach feel sick. This was certainly nothing like roaming the well-manicured, weedless lawns at Mount Kisco!

Still, I began to learn all kinds of new things about a world I never knew existed. There were dancing schools called Miss Somethings to which girls with family names like Holding or Rockefeller were invited, and there were places called Boarding Schools—also Miss Somethings or Other—which half my new class left high school to attend. These were schools where girls said goodbye to their beloved governesses and lived full-time for most of the year—an incomprehensible thought. There were also shiksa camps near Tripp Lake Camp that seemed to include many very athletic-looking blond-haired girls. Except for the one with which Tripp Lake competed, I had never heard of any of them before. There were clubs in Palm Beach that wouldn't allow Jews on the premises, even for lunch. And there was a racquet game called Squash, which sounded to me like one of the vegetables that Kitty forced me to eat. For the first time in my life I felt left out and confused.

My athletic abilities, however, rescued me once again and I managed to be accepted into the "alpha" group in my class. The dreaded house parties continued, but I found one friend who seemed to understand my anxieties—even though her ancestors came over on the Mayflower three hundred years before my own family schlepped to America. Her name was Mary and she was almost as sweet as Fraulein, and I loved the way she spoke and how humble she was. We became inseparable (and later on, we ruled the school together).

One night at dinner I called Kitty "Mummy"—what most of my new Waspy friends called their mothers. "What did you call me?" she inquired, with her eyebrows raised—which was always a warning sign. "Mummy," I repeated nonchalantly, as if I had been saying it all my life. Kitty, who had never heard of such a name to call a mother, was incensed. "Mummies are dead people in Egyptian museums," she shrieked. "How dare you call me Mummy?" Thank God she had on her makeup, which tended to make her a bit nicer than when she was without it—not wanting a frown to disturb the pressed powder.

The transition from a progressive Jewish school to a traditional Waspy all-girls school was very hard. But I have to hand it to Kitty, it was the right move for me and proved to be a vital step in my growth as an individual and toward my future.

A number of amazing skills and values were acquired in the homerooms and hallways of this school. This is where I realized the importance of intellectual pursuit and gained a respect for great teachers who expanded and nourished our minds. This is also where I became a very serious student, graduating at the top of my high school class, becoming an honors student at college and remaining a prolific reader all my life. Above all, this is where I first developed a profound sense of public service and discovered the great gift of participating in our communities.

THE HOLIDAYS AND A
VERY MERRY JEWISH
CHRISTMAS TO YOU

The Temple was not a big part of my life growing up. We went once a year, if that—although I am sure Kitty and Irving went twice and I just didn't know about it. But Kitty sent me to Sunday school at the Temple since most members of the Gang were sending their kids there as well. I hated it from day one. First of all, weren't five days of school enough?! I wanted to see my friends or go to movies or the theater with Fraulein; I wanted to play with Blueboy. So I started getting huge stomach-aches and couldn't get out of bed on Sunday mornings. Kitty called me a "faker" and initially was very upset, but I would clutch my stomach very convincingly, roll around on the bed and threaten to throw up, until she finally relented.

In spite of our casual approach to observing Judaism, Hanukkah and Passover were big deals for my family as well as for the other families of the Gang. Both evenings of these holidays took place in the home of Morris and Esther with Morris running the events. Our family and Mimi's family were the only guests unless some relative from out of the state was in town. Kitty, Mimi and I would be wearing our latest outfits, and the men would be dressed in their finest dark blue suits.

When we entered the dining room the lights would be low, and other than the tall grandfather clock ticking loudly, there would be no other sound—even Mimi would be unusually silent, awed by the ambience. My grandmother always set a beautiful table, which would then elicit oohs and aahs from Kitty and Mimi. The best china would have been washed over and over and the silver polished so well I could see my braces gleaming in my knife. And, of course, at Passover, there would be the empty seat for Elijah. I would always try to imagine him in a long robe with a tall pole staring at everyone and never saying anything, but muttering bad things under his breath. Although Morris decided on the seating, I always quickly sat down next to my darling father, hoping they wouldn't make me move.

Hanukkah was much more fun because everyone got presents and the dinner didn't last all night. Passover, on the other hand, went on forever as everyone read the Haggadah—a thrilling book that tells the story of Moses liberating the Jews from slavery in Egypt. I had plenty of chances to shine since I was always the youngest reader and could ask the four questions—*How is this night different from all other nights?* etc.—which I would do loudly and with great facial expressions to see if I could get a reaction from Kitty.

Morris would go through all the rituals, dipping this into that and that into this, reading lines in a singsong voice. I was never sure whether he was reciting them in Yiddish or Hebrew—only that Roger, who seemed to know a thing or two about Judaism, was always urging him along. But it was Irving who was the very best reader with his low, harmonious voice.

When I turned twelve years old, I was allowed to sip the Manischewitz wine. Peter always sneaked more and more wine into his glass when no one was looking, breaking the rules, which he was beginning to do in school as well as at home.

The dinner started with chopped chicken liver and then matzo ball soup, which was fine, but the next course was the horrible stuffed derma—a traditional side dish for Passover that is disgustingly made with a cow intestine stuffed with a mixture of vegetables. I would slice it into pieces and shove them around my plate without taking a bite, keeping my fingers crossed that no one was watching. The main dish, usually lamb, was pretty good and I didn't need to pretend.

The best part of Passover was my competition with Peter to find the hidden Matzo. Whoever won would get $20, which seemed like a windfall to us children. In general, Passover was very memorable. But neither Passover nor Hanukkah was a match for Christmas.

Interestingly perhaps, my Jewish family considered Christmas to be the most important day of the year. Kitty would even postpone her winter departure to Palm Beach in order to be home. Early on, when the three families lived in Mount Kisco, I remember how magnificent the Christmas tree was, year after year—rivaling, in my young eyes, the one at Rockefeller Center. The tree would be surrounded by hundreds of presents—desks, bicycles, books, dolls, and one year, a worktable with real tools for my cousin. We would take great delight in each other's gifts; whenever Peter got something better, like a bicycle, he always shared it with me. And there would be Mimi shooting me dirty looks because she could see I also wanted the guns and trucks he had received—I knew not to take them when she was looking. But our all-time favorite Christmas present was Peter's set of toy soldiers. We spent hours lining them up in his room and playing war—in particular the American Revolutionary War where we could take turns being the American or British soldiers.

Years later, after I was married, I would hold the Christmas celebrations at my house—but under the direction of Kitty. The preparations would involve lots and lots of telephone calls between Kitty's house and mine. I know this because one year I got a deadly flu and was home trying to rest when the calls started. She would insist on paying for the maids. Paying for the maids was very clever on my mother's part: it allowed her not only to control every detail, but also to be in on any gossip about my husband and kids.

My Gentile husband never ceased to be amazed at my mother's level of interest and involvement in Christmas. He decided it would be a good idea to keep secret the fact that we went to the Heavenly Rest Church on Christmas Eve—the one Christian thing we did each year. I think he was afraid that Kitty might show up for that too.

Kitty never liked to give Christmas gifts; instead she would give copies of the Zagat restaurant guide and lots of money. And she made sure that all the grandchildren received equal amounts. But in fairness to Kitty, she didn't like to receive gifts either. For years when she came to my apartment to spend Christmas with me and my own family, she would give me back whatever I gave her. At first I was insulted and annoyed. Then I wised up. I began giving her things I wanted for myself. I did this for a few years, and then I decided instead of things, I would give her clothes in my size. This made my Christmas much happier because I would now receive both money from Kitty and the most perfect item of clothing.

"LANDSMAN?"

My family, like most of their friends, took family vacations whenever my school was on break: Palm Beach in the winter, and again, sometimes, in the spring—or if Irving and Kitty were being particularly adventurous, Bermuda or Nassau in the Bahamas. But the fun really began with an occasional early summer trip to Europe or Canada. A part of each day would be devoted to sightseeing—which was my favorite thing to do, but the major purpose of those trips was shopping. Of course.

That being said, the hotels were no less important. Once we were shown to our rooms, an inspection worthy of Scotland Yard ensued. The decor was scrutinized; beds were tested; and the view outside was considered—sometimes the room was found to be on a floor much too low. If by then Kitty hadn't already moved us out and up, closets were then opened; beds were peered under for the presence of possible little creatures; headboards and mattresses, too, were thoroughly checked for bedbugs. Kitty's little fingers busily swiped every surface, making sure not one speck of dust was found. Through all of this—during which I wanted to disappear into the walls—Irving would roll his eyes and sigh, but he didn't dare contradict Kitty since life would be much worse for him if she wasn't happy with the room.

For the final act, Kitty would remove a can of Lysol spray from her luggage and begin a thorough job of disinfecting sinks, toilets, and bathtubs. (To this day I can't use a bathtub, even in a five-star hotel, for fear that there might be a trace of a "ring.") The point of this seemed to be less about sterilizing the place and more about ensuring that someone else's germs had been totally expunged from the room—especially if that someone was not a landsman.

Landsman roughly means "a fellow villager": a stranger, perhaps, but still someone you welcome because you know they share a common connection in the country of your ancestors. In Kitty's vocabulary, Landsman meant someone Jewish in whom she could immediately trust and eventually confide. And this brings me to the part of those trips I didn't like.

Whenever we entered the hotel's dining room or restaurant (the same would be true of hotel lobbies and museums), Kitty would look around to scope out the place; her eyes would narrow with a flirtatious expectation of meeting a new friend, presumably someone wearing clothes made by one of Kitty's favorite designers. However, before she would speak to the person, Kitty would turn to Irving and utter the critical question, "*Landsman?*" Irving would then nod his head, and Kitty, to my mortification, would approach the fellow traveler and, in an intimate way, whisper "Landsman?" This provoked a number of different reactions—from acute embarrassment at being approached by a stranger with a strange question, to bewilderment on the part of a Gentile mistaken for a fellow villager, to rage at the audacity of the question by someone who was Jewish and knew what the word meant.

In any of these cases, Kitty would smile politely and move our little family group quickly into another part of the room. However, every now and then, the stranger would laugh out loud, happily, at the question and hug and kiss Kitty as if they had been best friends forever. Kitty and her new friend would then make plans to get together the next night for dinner or spend the rest of the trip with each other, reveling in their newfound friendship. I would overhear Kitty sharing confidences with her latest friend—often about how beautiful her daughter was going to be once she got off her braces and had her hair permed. Of course, after the trip, Kitty never saw any of those people ever again.

THE HOUSE THAT
EQUITABLE BUILT

Jewish family businesses in the 1940s through the 70s were a phenomenon that is very rare in today's world. Most of them died off or were sold because the fourth generation of family members did not picture living and working with their fathers and brothers 24/7. (In fact, many of the siblings in those families ended up in fights with one another over the distribution of the assets once the businesses were sold.) According to the Family Firm Institute, only about 30 percent of family businesses, Jewish or not, survive beyond the founder's generation, and only 12 percent make it into a third generation. This was also true of my family's business, the Equitable Bag Company; it lasted three generations and was then sold before a fourth generation could take over.

Equitable was the largest manufacturer of shopping bags in the world. The company also produced something called a multi-war bag as well as various plastic packaging, but it was its line of shopping bags that brought the company fortune if not exactly fame. From large department store chains to other major retailers to tiny mom-and-pops, everyone ordered the bags for their customers; at checkout, all one had to do was turn their bag over to see the name Equitable Bag Company stamped on the bottom.

But Equitable was more than a purveyor of shopping bags— it was the absolute center of our universe. The whole family revolved around the business. In addition to Irving and Roger, my brother and my two male cousins also started working at Equitable. As the only granddaughter, I was never invited into the company, and later it seemed that Morris had no expectation for my husband to join up either. "Joining up," just like the Army, was what it was all about for the men in the family, with the same rules of behavior and lines of respect for the senior officers.

My father, however, hated the business. He was on his way to completing law school when my grandfather demanded he join up—and my mother took to her bed until my father agreed. (The fact Irving also knocked out one of his law professors for giving him a bad mark is another story.)

Every day, Morris, Irving, and Roger would put on their expensive suits and homburgs and climb into their Cadillacs to go to the office. What went on all day at Equitable headquarters was never quite clear in my mind, but what went on each night was unforgettable. The major topic of conversation was always the business and how the day had gone. And without fail, Irving would have had some serious disagreement with Roger or Morris and often still be frustrated with them at dinner. Kitty usually sided with Morris who was after all her daddy and the big boss, which made Irving even unhappier. Since I adored Irving, I would often find myself biting my tongue during their arguments.

When I was eight years old I did feel compelled to comment on a different matter. "Why don't you put pictures on the shopping bags?" I queried, thinking of the posters at school. "You could put photographs or patterns or graphics that showed what would be in the shopping bags, like beautiful dresses at Bloomingdales." Kitty, who was dumbfounded at my brilliance, quickly picked up the phone and called her father and, soon thereafter, shopping bags became the decorative objects they are today. I was regarded as the family genius—although Mimi was never allowed to know it had been my idea, because she would have been furious at the thought that I might be smarter than Peter.

Several times a year Irving took me to the headquarters and main factory in Queens where I loved learning about the machines and watching the people work. I was the little princess in the factory and was awarded the adulation a true royal deserves which, of course, I humbly accepted.

After my father died, Morris sent a Cadillac every day for Kitty so she could go into the office for a few hours and earn some money. According to my spies, my mother spent the hours signing some checks and listening to the personal woes and ailments of the secretaries. I guess someone had to do it. At any rate, it helped to ensure that Kitty could continue shopping at Martha's—which was certainly worth a twenty-minute car ride to Flushing, Queens.

My mother receiving a salary from Equitable also had its downside. It unpredictably caused a momentary rupture in her and her sister's relationship. I remember that soon after my father died, my husband and I, along with my brother and his wife, went to see Kitty—we were worried about her living alone. We had no sooner arrived at Kitty's apartment than Mimi showed up. Without a word of warning, my aunt turned to my husband and sister-in-law, and said, "We're going to have a family meeting. You can leave now. You aren't blood." Cain and Abel came to mind, as I looked on flabbergasted. But that wasn't the worst of it; it turned out that Mimi and Roger were trying to kick my mother out of the company, and Mimi had come to manipulate her. I think Kitty finally saw her sister's true character.

Once Morris passed away and the time was right, Equitable was sold to a few moguls who then sold it again and it was run right into the ground. Although they benefitted very well from the sale, Kitty and Mimi felt the loss of the business and their morning telephone conversations would often dwell on how horrible life was without Equitable at its center. What they never discussed was Mimi's earlier attempt to hurt Kitty. In my family, even the merest hint of disloyalty would not be talked about.

The end of Equitable was sad for all of us, but we were also seeing the sales of many of the family businesses that other Gang
members owned at around the same time. My brother and the
one cousin who had remained at the company walked away
with enough money on which to comfortably retire. By then
it was obvious that the next generation would do other things.

MY BELOVED IRVING

I remember how much I loved seeing Kitty and Irving all dressed up when they were going to a party. Kitty's makeup would be carefully applied, her short hair expertly waved, and her feet squeezed into the latest chic shoes. But it would be my father in one of his good suits or tuxedos, looking especially handsome, who would fill me with delight. I also found it thrilling to watch my parents dancing together. Irving was a great dancer and Kitty would lean her head against his and look happy.

A short, muscular, handsome man with a wide smile (that lit up my life), my father took after the men in his family who had emigrated from Eastern Europe to California and New York. He was born in Brooklyn with a hilarious Waspy middle name:

Dupont. When his mother was pregnant she had taken a trip to Wilmington, Delaware, and saw the DuPont name everywhere—evidently she liked it. Whoever would have thought that Irving's middle name would one day be a link to his daughter's Gentile future!

When he was twelve years old his family moved to Hollywood, California, partly because of relatives living there, and partly—mostly, I suspect—because he and his siblings were able to train for swimming and diving in outdoor pools. His parents would eventually move back to Brooklyn, but not before Irving graduated from Hollywood High School where he won the State diving title, the National Outdoor Diving title, and some gymnastics national championships. After high school he entered the University of Southern California, and later transferred to Columbia University from which he graduated in 1925 and starred in drop-kicking on the football team.

Irving was entirely different from Kitty. Where she was intense, he was very laid back. Where she was often poker-faced, he had a terrific sense of humor and took great pleasure in telling jokes to his family and friends. Where Kitty was not openly affectionate, my father was warm and loving.

As a child I couldn't wait until he came home from work when I could jump into his arms and smother him with hugs and kisses. And every Friday evening, I would sit down beside him while he played the piano and we would sing together—more times than not something from the songbooks of Rodgers and Hart or Gershwin. He was an amazing pianist. He could immediately play by ear any piece of music he had just heard on the radio; he also composed a number of songs, one of which became #1 on *Your Hit Parade*. While he may have inherited his athletic prowess from his father, he surely gained his love for composing and singing from his mother who had been a member of the famous [Yiddish Theatre] family of Boris Thomashefsky (the grandfather of the conductor Michael Tilson Thomas). My favorite song of my father's was "I'll Wash and You Dry"—which obviously was not about him and my mother since no one was ever allowed in our kitchen where Katie the Cook reigned supreme!

I would love it when my dad took me to the paper bag factory in Long Island, but the most fun I had with him was when we lived in Mount Kisco. As soon as Irving came home from work, he and I would jump into the pool and he would patiently coach me on my swimming and diving techniques.

I don't think Irving cared where I went to school—that was totally my mother's purview. In fact, I don't think he ever thought about social class or Very Important People either. He was very secure and confident—probably as a result of all his athletic achievements—and very happy in his own skin. I remember there was a time when Kitty wanted to change country clubs so I could meet a better class of Jewish (mostly German-Jewish) boys—ideal candidates, to my mother's mind, for marriage. Irving put his foot down since the golf course at the club where we were members was much better than the other one.

I will never know how my father managed his frustrations about working in the family business and, at times, having to contend with Kitty's siding with Morris. But even if he found joy elsewhere—golf, his great escape—he continued to love Kitty. He affectionately called her "Freckles," since her face and body were covered with them; he would joke around and tease her, which she particularly liked—she always was a sucker for being teased by a guy.

KITTY THE IRREPRESSIBLE

After my mother died, I found boxes of things that she had saved over the years, such as my report cards, letters from camp, dozens of pictures, etc. Who would have guessed? Kitty certainly wasn't the sentimental type!

But one of the best treasures I uncovered was a diary written in carefully constructed longhand by Kitty. She and Irving had taken the SS *Bremen* to Cherbourg, France, to visit Europe—without Mimi and Roger, believe it or not! When this was exactly I'm not sure since the diary shows no year, but it must have been around 1932—long enough before the war that the German ship would not be a problem for Jews. In fact, it was probably my parents' honeymoon.

The diary, which the ship seemed to have gifted its passengers, included a map of the ship's destinations and lots of instructions and information, such as: *The tendency of all travelers is to take more baggage than is necessary. Unless you are traveling in out-of-the-way places, it is best to take the least possible amount of suitable clothing and accessories...* Can you imagine Kitty following this suggestion?

But the guideline that makes me laugh out loud: *Unless the traveler has a room with private bath it will be necessary to arrange with bath steward for a set time each day when you will have use of one of the bathrooms.* The idea of Kitty sharing a bath with strangers is hysterically funny.

In another section of the diary, titled "Interesting People Aboard," Kitty wrote down names of some of the people: Gratstein, Bachrach, and Metz—all Landsmen, thank God.

The boat sailed at 12:30 on March 9. According to Kitty, there were "Loads of people down to see us off - gorgeous gifts. I wore my new beige suit from Martha's. I cried when I had to say goodbye to everybody on the dock." I can just visualize Mimi and Esther bringing flowers and gifts and cookies as farewell presents.

At the beginning of the trip, Kitty was very proud of not being seasick and seemed to be having a wonderful time. She danced; she played ping-pong; she played pool and bet on horse races—and was very proud of Irving winning $2. Irving, she noted, played the piano at night. She spent time with the

Bachrachs—"lovely people from New York." *And* she "Stayed up that night with Mr. Metz."

One of the most interesting parts of the diary includes multiple references to Mr. Metz, a corporate mogul, whom Kitty seemed to have met soon after the ship sailed. Who was he and why was he alone? Did Kitty have a crush on him? Did she fall in love with someone else shortly after getting married?

Things began to go downhill on March 11, several days into the journey. Kitty got a terrible bout of seasickness and a terrible cold. The ship's doctor thought she had tonsillitis. She took all her meals in bed and Irving was scared. But then there was Mr. Metz again: "Mr. Metz sends gorgeous roses." (uh huh!)

She remained sick for the next few days, with several calls to the doctor. She was finally able to move outside to her deck chair and get some fresh air, and there was Mr. Metz giving her the addresses of all his homes around the world. (*Irving where were you?!*)

The ship finally docked. Kitty said goodbye to Mr. Metz and she and Irving went through customs in one piece. Kitty seemed to have recovered and they travelled on to Paris, where they had a good time. But on March 15 she became sick again, and called several doctors. Back to bed. Irving brought her some French magazines, which of course, she couldn't read, but she "had a lot of fun trying to talk French to the chamber maid" and "Dad" sends her a cable.

March 16 and Kitty was back in great form and got her hair washed, cut and set in Antoine's, the famous Parisian beauty salon. "Hair looks gorgeous." Then off she and Irving went to the famous men's shop Sulka "where we almost bought out the place," and window-shopping down the Rue de la Paix. Obviously, Kitty was in heaven. Everything was going well until they got to the rotisserie where Kitty had a terrible nose-bleed, almost a "hemorrhage." I imagine Irving longing for a golf course, but maybe I am wrong.

The diary ends there.

Mr. Metz aside, I'm convinced that my mother did love my father even though she never showed any real affection toward him in public—or at home. They were a team and did every-thing together. They were equally concerned about my brother and me, and I could hear them talking about us at night. They seemed to have a good marriage and were great friends. But there was one man who forced my father to take a back seat his whole life, who meant the world to Kitty.

Kitty was in awe of her father. She was definitely Daddy's little girl and called him "Dad" with the utmost respect. She would run to get Morris anything he needed and never made any major decisions without his input. And Morris would respond to all this love and caring with lots of presents and money. He would pay for expensive dresses and jewelry. (I know he would also secretly pay for a lot of my clothes when Kitty went over the budget my father gave her.)

While Kitty deeply revered her father, she was nevertheless devoted to her mother. Esther was the sweetest of ladies (I loved my grandmother). Kitty and Mimi were very close to Esther, and they included her in on almost everything they did. They would talk to her every morning, seeking her advice. Esther was the glue that held the family together; she was the head mediator and negotiator for family squabbles, the matriarch whom we all loved and respected.

SHOP TILL YOU DROP

The telephone in our apartment at the Dorset would start ringing at 8:30 a.m.—after the husbands had gone to work—to plan the day's activities. Since there was no such thing as a conference call when I was a child, the logistics often became quite complex and rather comical. For example, once Kitty and Mimi decided on a time to meet and go to Martha's—the priority for them on any given day—one or the other would then call their mother. If Esther had a problem with the time, the whole scene would play out in reverse: Esther would call back Kitty or Mimi, who would have to call the other. If Mimi suddenly remembered that she had a hairdresser's appointment, the calls would start over again—and on and on it would go. Sometimes this dance of conversations would last well into mid- or late morning with no one going anywhere. This was intellectual and emotional foreplay for the event to come.

The important thing about shopping was not only the gorgeous designer clothes about to be viewed and bought, but choosing what to wear to the store. Clothes with mix and match possibilities were laid out on beds in the three apartments and serious decisions were made. Following the choice of outfits, make up was carefully applied to the face and neck as the excitement mounted.

The fact that this event took place at least once a week never diminished its importance. My grandmother, mother and aunt would meet in the lobby. Excited conversation would commence and continue in the Cadillac, chauffeured by Henri, all the way to Martha's door.

During the ride, Mimi would inevitably have something critical to say to Kitty who lived in awe and fear of her younger, more beautiful mean-girl sister. The truth is that even as Kitty and Mimi were totally spoiled and overprotected by their parents, the sisters' own relationship was complex. Kitty cherished her sister and would often say that she wished she was as pretty as Mimi; Mimi on the other hand was jealous of Kitty—of her popularity and even, later on, of her having the family's only granddaughter: me! "You have a big black piece of food between your two front teeth," Mimi would, for example, point out, gleefully, making Henri in the front seat grimace. Kitty would immediately rustle through her Gucci handbag to find a mirror and remedy the problem. And so it went until they arrived at the store.

Then the glorious pleasure of trying on dress after dress, coat after coat, pants and blouses, black tie gowns etc. etc. began. Martha was present, of course, explaining the beautiful details of each outfit, the ease of the zippers, the delicacy of the lace, the sheen of the satin. And afterward, there would be a serious conference among all three ladies and Martha with regard to the total cost of the purchases and which outfits might be given up—usually nothing.

The trip home involved exhausted post-climactic pleasure, with each woman dreaming of how she would look in each purchase and to what event she would wear each dress.

I absolutely hated being dragged along on these shopping trips—especially when I was the main object of the shopping. I would try on dress after dress, wanting the whole thing to be over with and wondering why I needed any of this stuff anyway, especially going to a high school where all we wore were uniforms. But shopping I was made to do on weekends—after all it was the *vocation* of the women in the family and I was not allowed to be an exception. Back at home, I had to try on each dress and parade in it before my father—who could have cared less but would nod his approval at each outfit while asking Katie the Cook for another double scotch.

MIRROR, MIRROR ON THE WALL

The essential complement to wearing designer clothes was, of course, having your hair perfectly done, and everyone at Kitty's hair salon completely adored her. She was by far their favorite customer, and they looked forward to washing, coloring and primping her every week—undoubtedly because my mother was friendly with every single one of the employees, from the stylist to the hair washer to the person who swept hair up from the floor. She also was just as chatty with all the other clients.

For Kitty, her salon was her club. For me, there was no escape. As uncomfortable as I was shopping with my mother, I was even more horrified going to the beauty parlor. Kitty would drag me there not only to keep her company, but also for my own remake—a cut or a perm.

Getting a perm was the worst. My hair was strangled in tiny little rollers all over my head and then drenched and cooked in a foul smelling liquid, which continued to stink for at least an hour. Then my hair was washed and set on large curlers to prevent the perm from becoming frizzy—that is, until I washed it a few days later and I looked like I had put my finger inside a light socket. Why this represented a more beautiful "me" to my mother, I could never understand; but as we left the salon, she would smile with satisfaction and continue to be nice to me for the rest of the day.

Kitty would hold court with the manicurist and pedicurist as well. Having her nails and toes painted were, in fact, her most favorite part of every visit; she would even bestow on me the privilege of helping her pick out a color—although I realized much later that she had already chosen the color for the day.

During our visits, one thing was guaranteed: that Kitty would find time to entertain everyone—the staff and the other patrons—with details of what had gone on with her since her previous appointment, including, to my embarrassment, stories of my accomplishments—particularly how many A's I had gotten on tests. Luckily her salon had a primarily Jewish clientele, so Kitty felt completely at home and didn't have to whisper the dreaded "Landsman" to the new clients.

Over the years, the venue of Kitty's club would change as she went from one to another; usually they all had French names. (It always surprised me how perfectly she pronounced their names since she had never learned a word of French.) The status of her beauty parlors was paramount. We ended up in a lot of salons with Very Important People, whose names, titles, and husbands' businesses Kitty would recite to me in a whisper when, hopefully, no one was watching.

Unfortunately, Kitty went through a stage when her originally dark brown hair got redder and redder. "How does this look?" she would inquire when we got in the cab after one of her color sessions, flicking her head back and narrowing her eyes in a flirtatious way. Each time I would find a different, wonderful adjective to use, while thinking to myself that she looked like Lucille Ball in a wind machine.

When we got home from the salon, Kitty would immediately call Mimi and then her mother to report on what had gone on at the beauty parlor and who was there. Post-salon gossip was the best part of the adventure, Kitty always said.

Decades later, I was mortified to discover that I acted the exact same way in my salon of choice. Everyone was my good friend to whom I would boast about my kids. I would pass around pictures of my gorgeous grandchildren, making sure that one and all got a good look. I even went further than Kitty, speaking French with the hairdressers and revealing intimate family secrets to those who set my hair.

Mirror, mirror on the wall, I am my mother after all!

FIXER-UPPER

One thing Kitty, and most of the other mothers in The Gang, had no hesitation about was having their kids operated on. This may have been especially true of upper middle class Jewish mothers of this era because they were overprotective of their kids, had more fear about medical issues and were financially able to afford the operations. Scraped knees and bee bites were also sources of great anxiety and much discussed.

I think I have had about eighteen operations in all, several of them during my childhood. My favorite was the second operation I had: a tonsillectomy. In those days it seemed like all the Jewish parents were having their kids' tonsils removed as a matter of course, a rite of passage—I remember Peter and I fiercely debating whose operation had been worse. But in truth it didn't hurt that much. I loved that operation because for many days afterward I was only allowed to eat ice cream—the only painful part was having to decide between chocolate and vanilla. (I would explain this to my grandson decades and decades later when he learned he needed to have his adenoids taken out and was so upset.) I also got lots of presents. In fact, I not only received a ton of sympathy and gifts for each surgical procedure, but Kitty was very, very nice to me, before and after, as well.

The first surgery was far less fun. Up until I was about seven years old, because of a weak muscle, my eyeball would slide to the corner of my eye and make me look like a crazy kid. That, of course, bothered Kitty terribly and had to be fixed, and so off I went to Mount Sinai. For a period after the operation I couldn't see, but Fraulein would cuddle me in bed and read aloud some of my favorite books.

The third operation was more serious than either the first two. I had been having stomach pains, especially on Sundays when I was supposed to go to Sunday school; naturally, Kitty thought I was just a "faker" (one of her favorite words). But one day I woke up screaming with a severe pain on my right side. I was rushed to the emergency room where they discovered I was suffering from acute appendicitis. Kitty felt terrible about having questioned me. The appendectomy was certainly not an operation I particularly enjoyed and the recovery took too much time away from sports.

Most of my other operations, such as a rotator cuff repair, were uneventful and took place when I was in my teens and older. But it wasn't all about the operations.

It also seemed as if I was always hurting myself as a kid. Sprained ankles, broken wrists, tears in the knees: these were all par for the course. I would come home from camp covered with ugly bruises everywhere. I used to count them proudly, while Fraulein swooned with sympathy.

Even with my numerous visits to the various hospitals, it still left a lot of time, it seemed, to spend on my teeth. The first orthodontist put on huge heavy braces that I had to wear for about two years and looked so terrible that I tried never to smile. After hours of practicing in front of the mirror, I miraculously managed to achieve a certain happy look with my mouth closed.

Sadly, that first guy apparently didn't know what he was doing, so we had to start all over again with a second orthodontist. He gave me nicer braces, but it took another four years. So while all my friends were starting to flash bright smiles with their new mouths, I was still trying to look happy with my mouth closed.

Growing up, I also had my share of plain old colds. They were okay—except when I got the croup and had to stoop over a horrible croup machine with a hose blowing vapor into my face. However, with a cold—particularly when I was in grade school—I could stay in bed for a week and read all my books and play all my games with Fraulein, who would hover about me with her forehead furrowed with worry. There were wonderful books with mazes and puzzles, which I loved, and Kitty would even come into the room once in a while for a game of checkers.

Maybe all Jewish mothers were critical and discouraging when things were good, and loving and sympathetic when their kids were sick or in trouble, but I never discussed this roller coaster of emotions with the children of the other Gang members, so I don't know. Thankfully, I had Fraulein to provide me with everyday maternal sweetness, to be my one constant—and that seemed to be enough for me.

MOVING TO FIFTH

The Dorset on 54th Street was terrific, but it was not classy enough or near enough to Temple Emanu-El on Fifth Avenue, where my grandfather wanted to make a big splash. In the 1950s Fifth Avenue, from 61st Street to 79th Street, was having a rash of new development; white brick buildings were built and made affordable, particularly, to a whole group of Jewish families who wanted the cachet of living on The Avenue. So, when I was eleven years old, Morris packed us up and moved our three families into three apartments on Fifth.

My grandparents' apartment was the smallest of the three, but I think I loved it the most. It had views of Central Park and you could watch the seasons changing through the windows. I loved the living room, which was beautiful and comfortable and filled with gorgeous antiques. There was also a book stand on which were displayed old books with pictures painted on the edges of their pages. I would lovingly stroke these books and dream of owning them one day. (My baby cousin Stevie got all of them!) And I loved Morris's office—I was always hoping to have the courage to pretend I had to go to the bathroom, and then run into his office to look for that famous money machine. I never dared to do this.

My own family's apartment wasn't all that big either, which meant that this was the end of Fraulein sleeping over. She could no longer bathe me at night or make sure I went "poo-poo" every day. That was a dramatic change for me, but little by little I began to see the upside.

I loved my room. First of all, it was next to Kitty's so I could tell when she was in a good or bad mood. Secondly, if I opened the window and leaned halfway out, dangling from my waist, I could see a few trees in Central Park. Also, I could spend hours sitting in the window, listening to Frank Sinatra and daydreaming about sex and romance—but only when Kitty wasn't home. My mother hated drafts and she would come into my room every morning, while I was still sleeping, to check if I had opened the window during the night. If I had done so, she would close it. Of course, her little process would wake me up since it was usually accompanied by lots of heaving, sighing and bitching.

My room had a big white desk and a beautiful mahogany secretary where I kept *The Little Princess* and my other favorite books. The wallpaper had big roses and other flowers, the rug was black with red and pink roses, and the chair was pink.

My bed was everything to me. It was the place where I read all my books and where Fraulein, who still came on the weekends and on vacations, could brush my hair for hours, murmuring complimentary things about how beautiful I was.

This was in sharp contrast to Kitty who, in rare moments of kindness, would sit down on my bed and, after telling me I had wonderful eyebrows, outline what needed to be done to the rest of my face—particularly braces and contact lenses— to match the perfect eyebrows. My immediate response was to run into my bathroom. Squinting my eyes I'd pretend that I was Laurie, the fast sex bomb in my class—only to emerge, feeling like a B-movie actress on a very bad day.

Sometimes I would go into the library for a little shot of the televised McCarthy hearings, which thrilled Kitty to an extreme—I think she was secretly in love with Roy Cohn. Also, on TV every Sunday night was "The Ed Sullivan Show"; I loved the show and couldn't wait for the guest appearances of the stars, especially the comedians. I often imagined taking a break from studying and, standing in front of Ed Sullivan's micro- phone, describing Kitty.

Kitty herself was very excited about our apartment, which was decorated by John Gerald, a brilliant and well known interior designer who did my grandparents' and Mimi's apartments as well. The living room had chintz curtains and velvet sofas and a wonderful reclining leather chair for my dad. The dining room had long red curtains and a beautiful crystal chandelier. It was a great apartment for entertaining and Kitty took full advantage of that.

People would come for dinner and bridge. There was much noise and much smoking. I would be paraded out in my latest dancing class velvet number from Martha's—and quickly learn the value of personality and sales. If I was very, very friendly to Mrs. Rosenstein and other Gang members, Kitty would be nice to me for a whole week.

Generally I liked the whole Gang—many of whom had also moved to the new buildings on Fifth and were always guests at Kitty and Irving's dinners—except for Sylvia. She was one of the ugliest people I had ever seen. Her face could have been a successful Halloween mask and she always wore black lace. I was sure that if I looked like Sylvia I would surround myself with hairdressers and makeup experts so I would never have to look in the mirror—but no, not Sylvia. Our apartment had a huge mirror in the living room that covered the biggest wall, and Sylvia would always sit opposite this mirror and look at herself during the entire cocktail hour. After dinner, when everyone would move back into the living room to play bridge, Sylvia would conveniently plant herself opposite the mirror once again.

As for bridge, I never thought of my mother as a real bridge player, but thinking back I realize she actually played a lot of it—especially with other members of the Gang. While they played, I would often notice what a little flirt my mother was. She had a way of smiling at the husbands of her friends, while she dangled her cigarette enticingly from her right hand. Whether this went over with the guys or not was hard to tell, but it was a fascinating side of my mother that I loved to watch. As an adult, I have often wondered if this is the way she acted with Mr. Metz.

Even though our three families were again ensconced under the same roof, gratefully (for my ultimate sanity), Mimi's apartment, along with Morris and Esther's, was on the other side of the building, reached by a different elevator. So communication continued, as it had been at the Dorset—mostly by telephone, the women constantly ringing each other up throughout the day and evening. But we had finally made it to Fifth Avenue— the Turner Towers in Brooklyn seemed a distant past.

THE COLLEGE YEARS

In high school I had my heart set on getting into Smith College, as did my best friend Mary. We would do our homework after school in my bedroom and, once in a while, we would open the window—yes, the same window that Kitty demanded I keep shut yet gladly opened for Blueboy—and contemplate how we would jump if we didn't get in. Fortunately, for the people walking below our building, Smith accepted both of us.

My four years at Smith were the freest and happiest years of my life. From the minute I stepped through the college gates I loved everything about the college. The campus was gorgeous and any time I had some space in my schedule, I would walk down to Paradise Pond and sometimes around it. It was said that if you walked around the Pond three times you were guaranteed not to be an old maid; but, much to Kitty's distress, I never made it around that many times.

At the start of each year, Kitty always brought rugs and blankets and curtains so that my college room was pure domestic perfection—one of my college roommates still remembers walking into our beautiful room and instantly feeling right at home. But Kitty was never satisfied with decorating just the surfaces; she would then spend time making sure that all the hangars in the closet were the same color and style, and placed in such a way that the clothes all faced in the same direction.

My freshman house was one of the smallest on campus and I made some good friends, although my roommate and I weren't particularly compatible. I had inherited Kitty's neatness craze and my roommate was very sloppy, so I finally tied a string down the middle of the tiny room to divide my area from hers. (The fact that we have remained good friends to this day, in spite of all that, is incredible.)

There was also a very threatening freshman who was about 6-foot-2; she wore a huge silver cross and tried to convert my roommate and me to becoming lesbians and Christians—in that order. We both moved out of the house after our freshman year and I was able to transfer to a bigger house where many of the athletes lived.

In addition to my studies, I had thrown myself into sports, especially volleyball and tennis, and became one of the outstanding freshmen who ended up being celebrated in canoes on Paradise Pond. I sailed through courses that seemed extremely easy after the ones I had taken in high school; I picked sociology as a major so I could go to Paris and Geneva on the Junior Year Abroad program.

Since one of my summer camp counselors was the Director of Athletics at Smith, I was commanded to join the synchronized swimming team. Although this meant diving into a freezing pool at 6 o'clock in the morning and going to classes with icicles for hair during the winter months, I still loved it.

During the early 60s the composition of students at Seven Sister Colleges was mostly 65-70% from private schools and the rest from public schools. A lot of the Smith students had been to boarding schools, many of which still emphasized decorum and manners. Most of the private school kids hung out together and were very preppy in their dress, and I was no exception: kilts, Shetland sweaters and knee socks! The boarding schools also produced many of Smith's athletes with whom I formed a genuine camaraderie.

But I was friendly with everyone. It was second nature to me to be as diplomatic as possible—perhaps living under Kitty's thumb had at least taught me that. And so my "hi-with-a-smile" won votes all over campus, and I ended up being Sophomore Prom Chairman—although I shamefully left my college roommate with a huge debt from the party as I sailed off to Paris the next year.

* * *

My junior year abroad in Paris and Geneva was incredible and the only year of my life I experienced total freedom—no mother, and no responsibilities except to go to class and not get in trouble. Of course I was bound to get into trouble since I sneaked around after curfew to meet my boyfriend. But I managed to pay off the concierge of the hotel where I lived the first semester, with the money that Esther sent me every week—so I thought I was safe. Much to my surprise, at the end of the school year, the professor who was in charge of the group called me into his office. He said he knew everything I had been doing, who I'd been seeing, what hour I came back to the hotel at night, and exactly how much I was paying the concierge to keep his mouth shut. (I still want my money back from that traitor concierge!)

Monsieur Over-the-Top, which we called the professor behind his back, assured me that if I hadn't been one of the best students in the group, he would have thrown me out of Smith and put me on the first plane home. But he loved heading the group and needed to prove that the students were doing well on the program, and I was the exemplary model. That was a close call!

At the beginning of the second semester in Geneva, my roommate and I pulled a fast one on Monsieur Over-the-Top. We were dying to live in a pension where we would have our own keys, could keep liquor in our room, and have absolutely no supervision. But there was only one such pension, and Monsieur decided who would stay with which families, and who would live in the pension; he asked us to write down our first, second, and third preferences. Knowing how perverse he was, we took a chance and put down three families as our choices and wrote a special note to him saying to please not even consider putting us in the pension because the family experience was the major reason we had come to Geneva. Sure enough, a few days later, Monsieur called us into his office to say that, although he was very sorry, he had chosen to put us in the pension. We wailed and moaned all the way back to our room where we closed the door, collapsed in happy hysterics, and pulled out a bottle of champagne that was hidden under my mattress.

As a final rebellion against our strict upbringings and Republican families, my roommate and I both became heavily involved with a couple of Communists—her boyfriend was Chinese and mine was European. Somehow Kitty smelled out this romance from across the ocean and informed me that she and Irving were coming over during our five-week spring break to do what was then called the "Grand Tour"—London, Paris, Rome, Florence, and Madrid. I had to cancel my vacation with my boyfriend who was a little out of sorts about this, and, after hearing all my stories, frightened to death at the prospect of meeting my parents. They were coming to Geneva before starting the tour and I wasn't too relaxed about seeing them myself. I took one look at my boyfriend's suits and dashed out to the best men's store in town to get him a fancy tie.

When Kitty finally met him she took a slow and thorough look up and down his shiny, threadbare suit and landed on the tie. Later, when I was yelled at for dating this guy who did not meet any of Kitty's standards, it was the tie that was the biggest outrage. "And you had to dress him up in a Hermès tie, as if I wouldn't notice the suit!"

Luckily for Kitty, my mysterious and smart but definitely weird boyfriend was not on my list of future husbands even though he did ask me to marry him after I returned to college the next fall. I have wished him luck and a darling mother-in-law ever since.

When I got back to Smith for my senior year I got into the honors program and spent most of the year immersed in my thesis, which focused on American attitudes toward Russia. It was, according to my honors professor, a flop since it didn't make the points strong enough, and it cost me my magna cum laude. I learned afterward that my two honors professors had been at war with each other about whether or not I should graduate magna cum laude. The senior of the two, however, won, and I graduated cum laude. I didn't get a chance to resent him for the rest of my life because he got killed in a car accident the summer after graduation. Was God angry at him too? I will never know. But Kitty and Irving, who were still disappointed that I hadn't found time to fit a nice Ivy League Jewish boy into my schedule, were thrilled when I joined the other honors students on the platform at graduation to receive our diplomas marked with distinction.

And so the next phase of my life began. The summer following graduation, I moved to Washington, DC, and shared a house with four other Smithies; we all had jobs on the Hill with congressmen and senators. Morris had gotten me a job with a Republican senator who was nice, but didn't share my ultraliberal views that were influenced by a communist boyfriend.

After my internship was over, I was considering going to law school when I got a job with the FCC. But instead of working with the lawyers, I was sent to the accounting department where I spent hours working on something called Promise versus Performance. The job consisted of counting the actual minutes of advertisements that a radio program included in an hour versus the number of minutes they had promised the FCC. This was a mind-numbing, horrible job, exacerbated by a miserable office environment with two of the accountants, who were in love, spending the days going in and out of their rooms (I was in one of them), and sending signals to each other by raising or lowering the blinds.

In addition, I had had enough of the bridge-playing Smithies in the house we shared and answered an ad in the paper from two young women who worked on the Hill and needed a third roommate. When I met them they were attractive and nice and I couldn't wait to move in. Unfortunately, one was sleeping with her senator and approaching a nervous breakdown, while the other one was in the throes of becoming the highest paid hooker in DC. This was the final nail in my future political coffin, but, luckily, that same fall I met Superwasp—he being a Mayflower descendant and all.

DATES, BOYFRIENDS, AND ONE FIANCÉ FOUND

I didn't date much during high school because my goal of getting into Smith College required 24/7 nonstop focus on my studies, with hours upon hours of homework. Besides, where exactly were we supposed to meet boys? I knew that the cross-town bus stops were the favorite meeting place for a small group of very blond and tilted nose classmates, but I didn't have the time or inclination to join them. Besides, I was more of a super athletic tomboy than a fast sex bomb.

Then there was Viola Wolff—the Jewish equivalent of the Miss Something's dancing schools to which I wasn't invited. But most of the boys came up to my shoulders or had pimples just longing to be popped. And these were the boys I was supposed to marry after college? There was a frightening lady called "Birdie" who would slam her cane on the ground whenever anyone misbehaved. I hated that place. I had one particularly expensive black velvet dress, which Kitty regularly forced me into for birthday parties and dancing school, but it wasn't as beautiful or as expensive as the dress of my friend Linda. Later on in life, Linda lied about Viola's to a group of New York women at a party we both attended and said that she had gone to Miss Something's Dancing School, a vicious betrayal of both Viola and her ethnic background.

But, back to boys. In my old school I had a terrible crush on Richard Fishman who had that long, lanky, pockmarked look of Clint Eastwood, with only a few pimples on his chin. He was the smartest boy in the class and, more importantly, the best athlete. I thought I'd faint every time I got near him. Later, when we both became Presidents of the Self Governments of our schools, there was a party for the class officers of all the New York private schools and we danced cheek to cheek, a highlight of my sex life then and maybe forever. When Richard was a freshman at Harvard, I invited him to the freshman prom at Smith, thinking we would then date during college and marry after graduation—although his father was *only* a dentist and I was already worried about the size of the engagement ring. And then he kissed me and it was horrible, a thin-lipped, dry and foul tasting kiss and, as Kitty always said, that was that!

I made up for my lack of social life in high school when I got to college where there were hundreds of mixers, blind dates, and a very pervasive network of Ivy League Jewish boys commanded by their parents to seek out Seven Sister (Ivy League equivalent) Jewish girls, date them and marry them after college. Pictures of these girls could be found in horrible freshman handbooks and they could be identified by their Jewish names. We all tried to find these books and destroy them.

Since my father, who had very traditional values, had made it clear that he was paying for college so I could meet one of these boys, I did try. But, instead, I ended up dating a Waspy guy from Amherst and then, more seriously, a Hungarian refugee and finally, and most thrillingly, the European Communist I met on Junior Year Abroad.

After the Communist, I met a gorgeous Catholic boy during my senior year of college. He was the best looking guy I had ever seen, but our first real date was a calamity. He picked me up at college since we were going to spend the weekend in Newport, where he was stationed in the ROTC, double dating with the friends who had introduced us. I was so nervous about the date that I spent hours applying tiny bits of makeup and choosing the right outfits. When they announced that someone was waiting for me in the hall of my college house I quickly finished my preparations and reached for a bottle of Chanel No. 5 perfume, which was all the rage. In my haste, however, I spilled the whole bottle over my neck and clothes, making me smell like a perfume factory. I didn't have time to do anything but meet him in the lobby. We kissed on the cheek, and I could see him looking at me in a very funny way. When we got into his car he inquired as to how much I liked perfume. So that was the beginning. About a third of the way to Newport I had to go wee-wee. Still very nervous and humiliated by the perfume incident, I grabbed some Kleenex, told him we had to stop, and did my thing behind a bush at the side of the highway.

Our "sleepover" was no less clumsy. Since he was a very good Catholic boy there was no chance of our doing the nasty, but the extra bed was in his room. I couldn't figure out how to put in my curlers without him seeing them. So, when I was sure he was asleep, I stuck them in and pulled the sheet over my head. In the middle of the night, however, I heard him get up to go the bathroom and I whipped out the curlers and brought my head out from under the sheets—only to stick the curlers back in once he had gone back to sleep.

That weekend should have been a sign of how the relationship might develop. Nevertheless, we liked each other and continued to meet. We had a few more dates, this time at Smith. He sent me recordings of all three Brahms symphonies, which I would play during torturous sessions of trying to perfect my senior Honors thesis. But then the Jewish thing raised its head, bringing our budding romance to an abrupt end. He said he wanted to introduce me to his parents, but when he told them I was Jewish they refused to meet me. Of course my parents, and certainly my grandparents, would have also refused to meet a Catholic boyfriend. In fact, my grandfather, in discussing my future with me, used to bellow, "No Catholics, never, never, never." I think that was a result of his having been in a lot of street fights with the Irish when he was growing up. Thank God he never lived to see my daughter marry her Catholic husband—there would have been a lot of trouble!

During college vacations, Kitty and other Gang members would hold conference calls or meetings to see whom they could dredge up for their daughters. I would go out with these guys no more than twice: because Kitty liked them and because—although they wined and dined me on their fathers' bankrolls—they didn't interest me.

There was this one guy, Michael, whom Kitty was mad about. He was about 6-foot-3 and very, very handsome, a Princeton graduate—and from a "very good" Landsman New York family. His family was very rich. (Kitty would always point out to me that there were a lot of fish in the sea so I might as well catch a rich one!) But Michael ended our dates with very awkward bear hugs in which my chin was crushed into his not too sweet smelling armpit. He would keep me there for what seemed like an hour. Kissing me seemed out of the question, which left me humiliated and peering at my face in the mirror after the date to see if Kitty hadn't fixed it up enough. Were the bottom teeth still a little crooked even after eight years of braces? Later on, I learned that Michael was gay and had died of AIDS. Maybe Kitty would still have wanted me to make a go of it. I'll never know. I do know that I spent a lot of wasted time in front of that mirror trying to figure out what was wrong.

Thus that fall, after my college graduation, Superwasp came along not a moment too soon. My college friend Sue introduced us at her wedding. I was a bridesmaid and was dating one of the ushers when Superwasp marched into the lunch reception and came over to me. I was immediately drawn to his blond hair and piercing blue eyes (which I was sure would be passed on to my kids and grandkids—but only our cat got the eyes!)—and allegedly he had been taken with my bright red suit. I learned that he was a Yale alumnus and a lawyer about to take on a very prestigious newspaper job. And he was a great athlete. In other words, Superwasp was perfect—except for his High Episcopal background and the fact he didn't come from a rich family (*which was worse*? I wondered). No matter. I thought he was adorable, not to mention I was entering a state of complete and total panic about becoming an old maid at the age of twenty-two. Such panic wasn't uncommon at the time. It would set in for most unattached young women in their senior year at college when their friends would be flaunting their huge diamonds in their faces and having long and boring discussions about their wedding plans. In fact, "ring before spring" was the main mantra for most of my classmates.

In the weeks that followed, Superwasp called me every day and we continued an argument that we had started at our friend's wedding about Betty Friedan's new book, *The Feminine Mystique*. Superwasp was trying to provoke me by saying the book was ridiculous; I violently disagreed. The heated debate went on for months until our wedding night when I finally admitted that I had never read the book.

When we had our first date at an overpriced restaurant, I proceeded to order the most expensive thing on the menu—how was I to know that he was still paying off his college loans?!

I introduced Superwasp first to my grandparents—it was the only time that everyone living in the same apartment building turned out to be a plus. I knew that Morris, who ruled everyone's roost, would like and admire him. He did, and immediately called down on the intercom to talk to Kitty. So, by the time we got to my apartment, both my mother and father were on board—here was a guy with a brilliant future. He eventually became a top media executive and the author of many articles on the First Amendment and a well-received book on a famous media case. He became an intellectual star and a law school professor.

Kitty did, however, give him her very slow up and down once-over, which had demolished the Communist-with-the-Hermès-Tie—but, after Communists and refugees, I knew she was relieved.

RING AFTER SPRING

What, with Irving complaining about my dentist bills and Kitty freaking out about the old maid stuff and getting my brother to fix me up with his friends, and Superwasp being so adorable, charming and seemingly on his way to being a Very Important Person, I felt like an engagement was in order. Even though he now claims to have wanted to ask me to marry him on the first date, I thought that Superwasp needed a little push.

So there we were in some huge mansion in New Jersey owned by the parents of one of Superwasp's best friends, and we were sitting on a couch (which was obviously designed and manufactured two hundred years before); we were necking a little—which was nice. In a pause between first and second base, I tried to find out how much Superwasp was making at the newspaper. "What would happen if we lived together for fun, what would be our budget?" I casually asked. We grabbed a piece of paper and filled in: rent, telephone, food etc., until we reached the amazing total of $15,000—his total salary—which, in 1963, seemed huge. "Wow," I exclaimed. "Have we forgotten anything?" When Superwasp replied to the negative, I jumped off the couch with joy.

"So that's it!" I was so excited I had to call Sue. "Okay" he said, a little bewildered, but wanting to keep me happy—so that maybe, just maybe, he could get to third base. I rushed to the phone and that was the beginning of our engagement.

In spite of his unfortunate religious background, Kitty was thrilled and immediately told Superwasp that she would go with him to Harry Winston to get the ring. When they got there she chose the perfect emerald cut diamond, which was the family diamond cut of choice and Superwasp proceeded to lose his life savings. That was their first adventure together.

Kitty's relationship with Superwasp would eventually settle into a fairly distant-but-respectful friendship, and, to my mother's credit, she would ask how Superwasp was feeling every time she phoned, which was almost every day. (I always hoped that was for the right reason!) And Superwasp, who had never met anyone like Kitty, got a great kick out of the things she would say and do.

Being the only granddaughter of Morris and Esther meant that all attention and resources were now focused on me and my wedding. The rabbi was lined up. The St. Regis roof was reserved. Unfortunately, Martha's did not have a wedding section, but Kitty, Mimi and Esther dragged me to many department stores and we ended up at the most famous bridal salon at that time in Bergdorf Goodman where I found the perfect dress. (I still have a picture of the gorgeous satin dress and Belgian lace veil that have somehow disappeared into the archives of some elite dry cleaner). Twelve bridesmaids and ushers were then selected. Bridesmaid dresses, sponsored by Morris, were chosen. Menus were decided on. Dance music was identified and paid for.

And then. My father died. Six weeks before the wedding.

SEA CHANGE

My father's death was the worst thing that ever happened to me.

Even though he was just fifty-eight years old, perhaps he had sensed he was about to die; the year before, he had started saying things like "I am packing in as many wonderful things in my life as I can" or "I am not long for this world." I thought he was just joking around, as usual, and didn't pay any attention to his feigned moroseness. In those days no one was very health conscious, so the pint of ice cream he devoured every night after dinner while watching TV didn't seem alarming, not to mention he was extremely athletic his whole life and excelled in every sport he tried—from diving, gymnastics, and football to playing golf and dancing. (According to family legend, my father's father was an early advocate of health and fitness, and the guiding force behind Irving's athletic achievements.)

But a month and a half before my wedding, my father had a massive heart attack. It was a damp March day, and he had just come home from his golf game where he had been trying to duplicate a score of 69 that he had made in Palm Beach a week earlier. All of a sudden, he clutched his chest and lay down on the bed. My mother immediately called for an ambulance; she and I were the only ones in the apartment, and when the paramedics arrived they asked me to help them with the EKG by attaching the electrodes to my father's chest. I was shaking so badly, I could barely manage it, and I was crying so much that I could hardly see through the tears.

The EMTs then rushed him to the hospital, with Kitty and I following closely behind in a cab. Our whole family started to gather: Morris and Esther, Mimi and Roger, and my brother, John, who had just left a date stranded at a restaurant. John and I went into the emergency room where we saw about ten doctors and nurses frantically working on our father, pumping his chest, hovering over him. We turned away in horror.

As we waited in the hospital I thought about how much my father loved the Brooklyn Dodgers (as well as St. John's basketball team)—it was almost baseball season and he should be getting ready to cheer the Dodgers on instead of being stuck inside this antiseptic place. But then a doctor appeared. He told us that they hadn't been able to save my father's life.

After Irving died, my grief was such that I was unable to look at a picture of him for ten years. Now I have several pictures of him in my office and love seeing his handsome face and his broad smile. Today, one of my biggest regrets is that Irving never knew his grandchildren, my children, both of whom were also national champions in their respective sports—one of whom was internationally ranked in tennis. My father would have been so proud!

ONWARD CHRISTIAN SOLDIERS

My husband and I celebrated our twenty-fifth anniversary at a chic club, which I had joined years before. There were about one hundred and fifty relatives and close friends, and the Peter Duchin band played. All in all, it was a very festive occasion. One of my college roommates, a minister, officiated the renewing of our vows. And then came the program. A famous anchorman was the MC and began with an announcement. He said that everyone should know that the National Conference of Christians and Jews had just awarded us a medal. This made us laugh, but it had a serious note. In that moment, I was catapulted back to the days leading up to our wedding and the day itself.

With my father's death, I was beset with guilt thinking about getting married so soon after. How could I feel that the world

131

had just ended, yet at the same time be excited that my life was about to start. The swings in my emotions left me overwhelmed, and with most of the wedding preparations already made I had no idea what to do. Together with my family, Superwasp and I decided to go ahead with the wedding. However, we moved the ceremony from St. Regis's rooftop to the hotel's library, and we cut out the bridesmaids and the ushers.

The senior rabbi had never performed a mixed marriage. Although there were some Jewish boys marrying Gentile girls, it was quite unheard of at that time for a Jewish girl to marry out of the faith. This resulted in our being interviewed by the rabbi and questioned as to how we were going to bring up our children when we lived in Scarsdale. My husband-to-be assured him that we weren't going to live in Scarsdale and that we would decide about the kids when they were in the picture. The rabbi was obviously disappointed with our interview, but followed it up with a very productive meeting with Morris. After the meeting, Morris immediately called up Kitty to excitedly tell her that the problem had been resolved and the rabbi would perform the marriage as long as Superwasp stepped on the glass and there was no minister within spitting distance. How did this happen? It turned out that my grandfather had agreed to "donate" a playground on the roof of the Temple and that settled it.

My wedding took place on a beautiful May evening in 1964. I was dressed in my gorgeous satin dress, with Kitty and Mimi and, thankfully, Fraulein fussing around me. A makeup man and hairdresser were both brought into the bridal suite to fix me up.

Relatives on both sides, a few of our best friends and, of course, members of the Gang were all present. Governor Dewey wasn't there, but Morris soldiered on anyway. And then came the big moment. As I was led down the aisle by my brother and feeling melancholic—not so many weeks before I could never have imagined doing this without my father—all of a sudden, outside the big St. Regis windows, the Salvation Army began blasting "Onward Christian Soldiers." On my side of the aisle there were many bewildered looks since many of my relatives and Gang members had no idea what was going on. But on Superwasp's side of the aisle people were trying to hide their smiles, and his friends and my brother-in-law were exploding in laughter. I didn't dare look at my husband-to-be to see his reaction. Clearly the rabbi knew the song and looked very annoyed with an I-told-you-this-wouldn't-work expression on his face.

Well, Superwasp managed to smash the glass quite successfully … and then came the vows. I had thought about this a lot. I had had a very privileged childhood and couldn't imagine becoming poor like the Little Princess; I also didn't like the "obey" part but knew I couldn't get away with too much. So when it came to "richer or poorer" I shouted out "richer" and cleared my throat immediately afterwards, thus never saying "poorer." The rabbi caught on and was about to correct me, but I managed to give him one of Kitty's dirty looks that would stop a vicious lion in his tracks. And so we got through the ceremony.

Kitty had decided to make the family of Superwasp into wealthy, upper class (this part was true) members of the Boston elite. The Gang was both awestruck and horrified—how could

I be going against my background and heritage?—but they were fascinated and charmed by Superwasp and his family. We made it through the reception and jumped into my brother's car since my brother was taking us to the airport so we could catch our flight to Jamaica, a popular honeymoon destination at the time. I thought John was acting very uncomfortably, and that it was actually very strange that he was the one driving us to the airport, until he told us that we needed to talk. Morris, he said, insisted on us calling Kitty every day during our honeymoon to report to her on how things were going and find out how she was. I thought Superwasp was going to explode with rage, but we just said "sure."

What did happen on the honeymoon, however, was never going to be reported. The remaining funds in my husband's life savings had been poured into renting a beautiful villa at a gorgeous resort with a swimming pool and tennis court. By the time the plane landed, however, I was in a tizzy about the whole thing. We had gotten engaged so quickly—on our third date!—and no one lived together in those days: *Maybe I was too young. What if I should have married someone Jewish? What if Superwasp were messy? What if Superwasp didn't want to pay my dentist bills?!*

By the time we got to the villa I was in a catatonic state. Superwasp couldn't wait to play tennis, however, so our tennis clothes and racquets were whipped out of our suitcases and we rushed over to the court. We had never played tennis together before and I was sure that I could beat Superwasp since I had been such a champion at clubs and camps. But he proceeded to kill me in the first set, after which I lay down on the tennis court and became hysterical. Through my sobs I could see Superwasp trying to figure out exactly what had happened and what was wrong with me? Years later, during a trip to Europe, we ran into a couple who had also been at that resort at the same time on their honeymoon, and they told us they had watched the whole scene from the bushes and thought it was the funniest thing they had ever seen.

Unfortunately, in my hysterical state, I was about to ruin the entire honeymoon, when I found a big wooden chest filled with paperbacks in the living room. So I read twenty books on the honeymoon and was very nice about everything else—except for the mosquitoes, which sent me flying around our hotel room with a rolled up newspaper at 2 a.m. Superwasp, who had no idea about my fear and loathing of bugs, was stunned.

Well finally, with tennis games getting more even, books being read and mosquitoes being killed, we had a great time. A memorable honeymoon if ever there was one!

We returned from our honeymoon to a tiny apartment on East End Avenue—there wasn't even a question that we would live in the same apartment building as Kitty and Irving and the rest of the family. To my surprise and delight, Esther had had the place decorated for me, and when Superwasp opened the front hall closet, hundreds of shopping bags fell out. "What the hell is that?" he demanded. "*That*," I replied, "are the paper bags my family manufactures." "Paper bags," he exclaimed. "I thought your family was in publishing and published paperbacks!"

By that point, maybe he was questioning what he had gotten himself into.

In spite of being engaged on only the third date and not knowing each other well when we got married, we have lasted more than fifty-five years with huge celebrations taking place not only on our 25th anniversary but on our 50th as well. Now, where is that National Conference of Christians and Jews medal?

BANANA TREES AND BREAKERS

When I was a child, early morning was my favorite time of day in Palm Beach. Fraulein would take me walking along the intracoastal waterway just as the sun was rising, delicately lighting the beautiful, big old wooden houses and the majestic trees that lined our path. I still find myself dreaming of those trees — banana trees in particular that seemed so exotic and palm trees swaying in the warm breeze — of the wonderful smells of the flowers the moment you got off the airplane; and of the views of the stunning ocean on one side of the island and the beautiful waterway on the other. Has there ever been a more perfect place anywhere else in the world?

Henry Morrison Flagler established Palm Beach in the early 1900s when he built two luxury hotels, the Breakers and the

Royal Poinciana Hotel, and built himself a mansion called Whitehall. Flagler got his rich friends to buy adjacent real estate lots, and together, they formed a close society whose favorite social activity was attending Henry's great parties at Whitehall.

It was often said that Palm Beach, at least in the past, had an invisible line intersecting the middle of the island at the spot where the Breakers is located. All the Gentiles lived on one side of this line stretching out to South Ocean Boulevard, and all the Jews lived on the other side including North Ocean Boulevard. I doubt this is true anymore, but it was certainly true in the 1940s and 1950s when my family, including, of course, Esther and Morris, Mimi and Roger and their kids, and the governesses would go down to Palm Beach for winter school breaks, and sometimes for the spring breaks as well. We would stay at the wonderful Whitehall Hotel in what had been Flagler's home and is now the Flagler Museum.

Henry Flagler would probably be turning in his grave if he knew that his beloved Whitehall had been turned into a Jewish hotel from 1925-1959. This came about since the Breakers and other hotels would not accept Jewish reservations.

In addition to the hotels, Palm Beach also had two famous Gentile country clubs. Because of the restrictions of these clubs, my grandfather and others founded the Palm Beach Country Club, which was as elite and difficult for a Gentile to get into as the Gentile country clubs were for a Jew. With its extensive and gorgeous facilities this Club soon became a favorite playground for my family and other members of the Gang who also vacationed in Palm Beach.

When Morris and Esther were in their seventies, they again bought three apartments—this time in the very Jewish Palm Beach Towers where many members of the Gang also had apartments. So Kitty and Mimi and their families could carry on living together in the same apartment building during the winter months when they were in Florida. The Palm Beach Towers had a restaurant and a hair salon and spacious cabanas where the Gang and my family continued their bridge games. The cabanas were always stocked full of delicious cookies, cakes and sodas.

After I had two babies, Morris would treat me and the kids, and the nanny, to a three-week vacation every winter at the Breakers Hotel (now desegregated) in Palm Beach. I would spend time with lots of my Gentile friends who would invite me to play tennis at one of their clubs. Since the guest fees were so expensive, my friends asked me to submit an application for a two-week guest card, for which I would pay. On the card I noticed a line asking for your religion. When I told my pals I was going to write in Jewish, they assured me that no one would know I was Jewish—particularly because of my Waspy last name. Needless to say, I refused to do that and stuck to the tennis courts at the Breakers, which were terrific anyway.

Coincidentally, Superwasp's Uncle Ben and his wife had a very big house on the Gentile side of the Breakers. Ben had a London taxi which he drove around Palm Beach, and was known to be a quite a character who loved to drink and party. So perhaps it was no surprise—even though he had refused to come to our wedding because I was Jewish—that Ben fell in love with my vibrant mother and invited her regularly for lunch at his exclusive, then-restricted club. This delighted Kitty, and her friendship with Ben became the source of much conversation and wonderment in telephone calls with Mimi and other members of the Gang. May the non anti-Semitic side of his character rest in peace.

Our visits to Palm Beach finally came to an end when our three-year-old son started counting Rolls-Royces, and my husband felt that was enough. And in the decade that followed, all those lovely old houses that once caught the early morning light were torn down, depressingly replaced by cement mansions erected behind stonewalls. Even so, I will never forget the way the place awakened my senses: the smells of the flowers, the sights of the banana trees and the sounds of the breakers on the sandy shore.

MY BROTHER JOHN

My brother, John, was handsome and funny and full of hell. He was eight years older than I so I never saw much of him except on vacations in Palm Beach. He was in his teens then, and I remember how fascinated I was by his flirtations. Inspired by some movie about a kid sister and the antics she pulled, I decided she was the perfect role model. While John necked with one of his girlfriends or another, I would hide behind the couch in the living room of our suite. After a few minutes, I would extend my arm and wave my hand in front of his face until he gave me a quarter to disappear. Despite my gleeful bit of dabbling in extortion, I never tattled on him. What those girlfriends never knew was that my gorgeous brother lined the bottom of his shoes with extra socks to make himself a lot taller and pretended to be two years older than he was to be closer to them in age.

In those days, I may have been just a bratty kid sister, but John never made me feel like a nuisance. He always gave me plenty of affection, and he was very proud of me when I got into Smith—although I secretly thought it was because all his favorite girlfriends were Smithies.

As siblings, we were opposites in temperament. Whereas my brother's approach to everything was pretty laid back, I was probably more impatient—ambitious both academically and athletically. For example, he was a swimming recruit for several colleges, but he dropped out of Dartmouth's swim team after his freshman year. That would have been impossible for me, particularly since my sports achievements made our father so proud.

In the meantime, our mother spoiled him rotten—their relationship was undoubtedly a good example of how close-knit the Jewish mother-son relationship could be. Once John went away to Dartmouth for college she could no longer overprotect him. Nevertheless, he was a dutiful son who would call his mother every day even after he was married.

When I was in high school, John entered the Air Force and was stationed in San Antonio where he fell madly in love with a beautiful model and asked her to marry him. The whole family, including Mimi, flew down to Texas, to meet her. Kitty was terribly upset by his decision to get married. The cause for this was simple: Janet wasn't a nice Jewish girl from an acceptable

Jewish family. And, as if to rub salt into the wound, Janet was a shiksa from a poor family.

After we met her and went back to the hotel, Kitty had fits and tantrums. I had to share a room with Mimi, which to my mind made everything even more horrible. Irving tried, unsuccessfully, to calm Kitty down. But in the end, John prevailed and he and Janet got married—after Janet agreed to convert to Judaism. (This set the stage and broke the ice for my future marriage to a Gentile who would never have converted to anything.) Kitty didn't fully accept Janet until she and my brother had three children, and my mother finally realized that her son's marriage was there to stay.

I loved Janet, although we were never confidantes. When she died in her early sixties of lung cancer, John became my best friend. In addition to his calls to Kitty, he phoned me every day and we would talk endlessly, particularly when he decided to get engaged to a Palm Beach shopkeeper who everyone in the family—except for my brother—thought was a gold digger.

John wanted me to meet her and told me to go to the Valentino Boutique in New York where she was trying on very sexy dresses to wear to her daughter's wedding. *Who does that?* I was thinking as I watched her. And when he told me how beautiful he thought she was, I informed him that I thought she looked like one of his beloved dachshunds. He was already tasting the stale cake under the icing, and I think that did it. To my relief and that of his children, he broke off the engagement; he finally found someone much nicer and more intelligent to marry.

At the age of seventy-six, my brother died from prostate cancer. I was devastated. My baby cousin and I were now the only ones still alive from my childhood family. I cried a lot! We had not only been separated by age but also by our life philosophy—his more in tune with the relaxed ambiance of his later New Mexico surroundings and mine keeping pace with the pressures of New York City. But I believe we loved and respected each other a lot and grew closer and closer as the years went by.

CHEAP GOYIM

When my husband and I were first married, in 1964, he decided he needed to get away on weekends from his demanding job and, since we both knew the area, we bought a house in Washington, Connecticut. (This was the town where I spent many weekends at the country homes of my schoolmates during my high school days, doing a lot of loathsome hiking.) Washington was then a community largely populated with very Christian names like Gibson, White and Van Sinderen. If you don't count one famous Wall Street financial wizard, who was at least half Jewish, I may have been the only Jew, at that time, to buy a house in that town.

The local real estate agent seemed delighted to meet us. In those days, real estate agents all across the country were very powerful in restricting communities to "acceptable" residents, and this agent was no different. As we drove around, he proceeded to point out parts of town where we wouldn't want to live because no "debutantes" resided there. His comment reminded me that the notion of my "coming out" was short-lived. When I was in high school Kitty received a phone call from another Jewish mother who said she could get me into the New York Infirmary, which was one of the most exclusive debutante balls. But Kitty, to her credit, said no, and put an end to that.

The real estate agent was clearly very anxious to have a couple with our very English last name buy a house in Washington. Therefore, when we passed a house on a beautiful piece of property with a mailbox that said Krinsky or Damrosch, he assured us that the people were "Russian, not Jewish!"

Finally, we pulled up to a house on a beautiful local lake that he had in mind for us. We immediately loved it—small and quaint as it was—and wanted to buy it from that very first moment. As we were getting out of the car, the agent told us that he had assured the owner that no blacks (not the word he used) or Jews would ever be allowed to buy the house. I shook my head, looked him directly in the eye, and told him that he had a problem because I was Jewish and we were going to buy this house. He turned purple in the face. Several months later I heard that he had collapsed from a heart attack and died. So much for that—we bought the house!

Aside from the real estate agent, we loved the community. The local club was, in fact, open to everyone in town and there was no enthusiasm among the residents for a country club with a pool. The Club did have a small shack on a beach that served as a fine, understated changing house with a fridge; it had been given to the Club by New York weekenders who had moved to the town at the turn of the century. They built large shingle style houses designed by a New York architect, Ehrich Rossiter. The houses eventually passed out of their hands and were picked up, as were many others, for a song by couples our age, mostly from New York City.

We couldn't have been more elated with our new home, and persuaded a number of our New York friends to buy houses in the area shortly after we did; they were mostly lawyers from well known New York City law firms such as Debevoise and Plimpton; Lord, Day and Lord; and Simpson, Thacher, and Bartlett. They were representative of a lot of lawyers from Wall Street firms, mostly graduates of Ivy League colleges and law schools.

With our own "gang," we would meet on the beach on weekends, with our kids in tow, picnic lunches, blankets and so on. There was no cooking facility and that's how we liked it. The only employees hired by the Club were lifeguards, who were local high school students.

I remember one summer, before we had children, Kitty came up for the weekend to see our newly decorated, tiny house, and to our surprise, she loved it and called it a beautiful little doll's house. We took her over to the beach to proudly share with her our beloved shack and have her meet our friends. Of course, we knew it was the complete opposite of the familiar Westchester Country Club—but that was the point.

Kitty took one look around, totally unimpressed with the shingled shack, the rustic beach chairs on which we all lounged, and our friends who were lounging on them. When we returned home I couldn't wait to talk to her about the Club, and was rewarded with a typical Kitty response: "The Club? Cheap Goyim!" That was my Fifth Avenue Kitty.

CHOP CHOP

As if Washington, Connecticut, and Palm Beach didn't have enough exclusive and restricted areas, Superwasp and I found ourselves in the same kind of community on Martha's Vineyard. Why was that? Because competitive tennis was our thing and a lot of the best tennis players on the island belonged to this club with a Chop in its name.

It was, and is, a terrific family-oriented community but, again, I seemed to be the first Jew to join the Club and participate in its activities. A famous Jewish opera singer had married into an old Chop family but she wasn't comfortable in the community and went back to an area up-island where she felt more comfortable.

One afternoon, as I was walking along the flowered paths of the property, one of the most important grande dames who controlled the Club came up to me and asked me how Carola was. I immediately knew to whom she was referring: Carola Warburg Rothschild of the famous and aristocratic, German Jewish Rothschild family. "Why do you ask?" I inquired, affecting bewilderment. "Well dear, isn't she your first cousin?"

True to form, I had to answer that I was not a member of the Rothschild or Warburg families but that instead, my family came from Flatbush, an area in Brooklyn. Thank goodness this nice lady—unlike the Washington, Connecticut, real estate agent—didn't keel over, and we became good friends in spite of my "landsman" background.

Another thing that eased my acceptance in the Chop was my tennis game. I won a fair number of tournaments and, thus, got my Waspy name splashed across the tournament winners' plaques, which decorated the walls in the building that became the church on Sundays.

The church did not prove to be a problem. I slept late on Sundays and then rushed out of my rented house to make it to the tennis courts, joined by the other people in the community who had attended the church services. In any case, I heard that there wasn't that much Jesus stuff in the church talks, just in the hymns—and I was even asked to give one of the Sunday talks, which I proceeded to do with great delight.

Of course things change. A few years later, while my husband and I were smashing balls at each other, on to the court next to ours came a rather thick-set man who did not have blonde hair and blue eyes—quite the opposite, and who had a cigar dangling from his mouth and a tennis racquet attached to his hand. My eyes opened wide in astonishment. Evidently, this pretty famous guy had married into one of the Club's oldest Boston families, all of whom were very blond and very blue eyed. So there it was, the beginning of the end for the Chop, which had always been populated by old, upper class families, mostly from Boston and Cleveland. Intermarriage had crept in.

The Club today has a diverse membership since it was the preceding generation—that of my mother's, both Jewish and Gentile—that didn't intermarry and wanted things to stay the way they had always been. But I am still very careful when I go there to visit, not to whisper "Landsman" to any newcomer.

HOCKEY SCHMOCKEY AND OTHER ICE STORIES

Marriage to Superwasp was great. I loved his friends from Yale. Like my husband, they were all attractive, athletic, very smart, and on the cusp of great achievement in their various professions. At this point, they too were happily married and starting families. We spent time together: dinner parties, week-ends, even some vacations. The group didn't exactly replicate the inseparable social life of the Gang, but it came close and was a lot of fun.

However there was one totally new experience in marrying Superwasp that I hadn't been aware of, a Waspy sport I had never even heard of in my Jewish childhood: ICE HOCKEY. Certainly none of the Gang or their children played this sport,

155

and if the professional ice hockey teams were popular then, I never knew it.

Superwasp and his brother had been stars on the Yale varsity ice hockey team, something that they and their teammates never seemed to get over. Maybe it was due to the crazy carrying on of the Yale students in the ice rink every time the team took the ice; maybe it was due to the macho competition and occasional fight. But whatever it was, they longed to continue it after college, and so they joined semi-pro teams and leagues in various cities. Superwasp's team was the Bronxville Bombers and they were tough and aggressive.

At first I was a little appalled by this sport. It was very rough. I had no idea what "icing" or "offsides" meant and no one seemed interested in spending the time to teach me. I took pleasure in seeing Superwasp come off the ice between periods, flushed with happiness and joy; even so the likelihood that ice hockey would become an obsession for me, seemed at best remote. Nevertheless the sport became a large part of my life.

After we bought our country place in Washington, Superwasp started a community hockey program for 300 kids; he went from house to house, knocking on doors to recruit the little boys, and spent a lot of time raising money to pay for uniforms for the kids who couldn't afford them.

I learned the rules and tactics of the game and started to get into it. I would yell and scream at the refs if I thought they were unfair to our team—to the point that I damaged my vocal chords and had to drop out of the, believe it or not, Church choral society that I had joined in New York.

So when our son, Tom, was born, he never had a chance. He had skates in his crib so he could get used to the idea. He started skating in Connecticut at three years of age and was playing hockey by the age of five. My husband was ecstatic. As Tom grew older, we would drop him at the ice rink with his little brown lunch bag so he could skate all day, and we had a warming house built so that he and his friends could warm up when necessary.

I became increasingly involved. I carried a big heavy cowbell to the rink and rang it loudly when we got a goal or the other team got a penalty. One day, when my son's team was playing another local team, some kid pinned Tom down and started hitting him. Since my favorite spot in the rink was behind the penalty box, I sat there fuming until the kid got a penalty for the fight, sat down right in front of me, and took off his helmet; then I raised my heavy handbag over his head and whopped him as hard as I could. Fortunately, no one saw this but my husband; unfortunately, I didn't knock the kid out.

And this was just the beginning. Since I was at every game, my husband periodically asked me to substitute coach when one of the coaches dropped out. I loved doing this and the boys loved me because I was constantly yelling at the refs if one of them got a penalty or was harassed by the opposing team. One day I went onto the ice to ask the ref to kick off a dirty player who was elbowing my players under their chins, making their heads snap back. I was in a rage, so the ref called the player over. She took off her helmet and swished her long hair in a circle. That shut me up. She was the only girl in the league.

Kitty was amazed at my involvement with hockey. "Why are you wasting your time doing all this and why in the world are you taking that child down to a freezing rink to skate at an unheard of hour in the morning?" When I told her how important this sport was to my husband she looked at me with eyebrows raised—again the warning sign. "Hockey, schmockey," she said. "I just don't understand it."

To my husband's great disappointment, Tom chose squash over hockey at prep school. But, thank you God, our other son took up the flag and was Captain of the Hockey team at Groton. (Yes, our kids were now going to the Waspy boarding schools that I had heard about in my high school.)

But the ice experience didn't end there. Since we lived on a lake, our daughter was also skating very well by age three and she went onto the ice in between periods at the hockey rink in the country. When she was about six years old, she won a figure skating competition at a rink in New York and a skating pro approached us and said he would like to take her to the next step. Unfortunately, this step involved getting up at 4 o'clock in the morning to get to the rink by 5 so she could skate a couple of hours before school, and even on the weekends. I still can't believe we did this, but she seemed to love it and competed in figure skating until she went off to Hotchkiss.

To help Kitty understand figure skating and her granddaughter's passion, I took the best box on the ice for the most important Skating Club event of the year. The best kids had solos. When Kitty, who had brought extra sweaters and blankets to keep from freezing, watched the first solo, she asked me who that was. "Joanna," I answered, "a friend of your granddaughter." She kept asking me the names of the soloists until finally our daughter came on to the ice. "And who is that?" Kitty queried. "That is your granddaughter" I answered, amazed that she didn't recognize her since we were only several yards away from her on the ice. "And how would I know that?" was Kitty's answer. "It's not as if you ever bring her to see me!"

ISRAEL

I took my daughter to Israel when she was a teenager. She was going to the Waspy Hotchkiss School, and I decided she needed to discover her roots. I organized the trip and arranged for a guide, an archeologist, whom a friend had highly recommended. Over the ten days that we would be in Israel, we were to travel from the Golan Heights, southward to Eilat, a popular resort located at the northern tip of the Red Sea.

The guide drove us in his van, and from the moment he started the engine I knew we were in for a very long ride. He was very pushy and annoying and never stopped talking. So, instead of my daughter breathlessly drinking in Israel and everything he had to say, she ended up sticking on her earphones, turning on her Walkman, and tuning him out for most of the trip.

Despite our guide's bumptious personality, my enthusiasm for the country wasn't dampened at all. I was completely blown away by the beauty as well as by the many hospitals, universities, monuments and museums that were built by Jews; Israel was breathtaking and I gained a huge respect for my people. The fact that Israel was only ten miles wide in its middle, and surrounded by Arab countries, made me realize the fear that the Israelis lived with every day.

We stayed overnight in a kibbutz in the northern part of the country. This was an amazing experience but a little scary since we were so close to the Syrian border. I couldn't understand how the children lived separately from the parents, but otherwise I was intrigued by the life in a kibbutz and the general philosophy.

When we got to Jerusalem, our guide took us into the old city to visit the Jewish Quarter, which was beautiful and fascinating, and then he took us to the Arab quarter where the first intifada was just beginning. I could see gangs of Arab boys in leather jackets, wielding sticks, and was so angry with the stupid guide that I could hardly speak. But he assured me that he was very friendly with the Arabs and no one would get hurt. Even so I screamed at him to get us out of there, and made him go first, then had my daughter go next, and I followed closely behind; that way my daughter would be protected. That was the beginning of the end of the guide. When we reached the Dead Sea, I fired him—afterward my daughter and I made our way down to the bottom of the country by ourselves.

One thing I will never forget were the Jewish maids in the hotels. I had never before, and have never since, met a Jewish maid. In my experience, the Jews hired the maids and they were mostly German or Irish. Of course this was Israel, so there were bound to be Jewish maids, but it still astounded me.

Although Israel didn't have much of an effect on my daughter, I think it changed my life a lot. I eventually joined Temple Emanu-El, where Morris and Esther and Kitty and Mimi had long been members, and got Kitty to name one of the steps to the Bimah, on which the rabbi delivers his sermon. So now our family has the playground, the Bimah step, and the flagpole—which Mimi gave the Temple since it was outside and had a lot of visibility!—named after us.

OY VEY, I'M GOING TO CHURCH

Kitty saw both of her children marry Gentiles. My brother broke the ice with his marriage to the shiksa model, so when I brought home Superwasp, whose only drawback was not being Jewish, things were much easier. And it didn't end there; the assimilation continued with her grandchildren. All five of them married Gentiles! By this time Kitty was in a permanent state of shock and didn't utter a sound of protest.

Kitty's first encounter with Christian icons was in Santa Fe where my brother was living. Crosses were sold everywhere, in the marketplace and in charming little boutiques. When my brother opened the door of his new house to proudly show Kitty how wonderful it was, there were at least twenty beautiful crosses on the wall of the entryway. I happened to accompany Kitty on this trip and she couldn't wait to pull me aside and ask just what my brother thought he was doing by putting up all those crosses. She was agitated to say the least, and I had to spend a lot of time explaining that the crosses were considered to be works of art that everyone wanted to buy and that many of them were worth a lot of money. Kitty instantly calmed down; she liked that!

But that was not the end of the crisis. My brother's son moved permanently to Connecticut where he bought up acres and acres of land and became a very sophisticated farmer. The town he moved to was close to Washington, and was settled in the eighteenth century by Puritans who built not one, but two congregational churches in the area. When my nephew became engaged, he and his fiancé picked one of the two congregational churches to get married in.

My husband and I drove Kitty to the church for the marriage ceremony. Kitty was nervous and uncomfortable, fingering her pearls and muttering a few incomprehensible things under her breath. To try to comfort her, Superwasp cracked jokes and also explained how the Puritans came to the United States to separate from the Anglican Church. He left out the part of being, himself, a descendant of the doctor on the Mayflower, because he thought she had enough to absorb that day in Connecticut. He talked about how the Puritans, and then the Congregationalists, wanted the power of the Church to be in the congregation, not the priesthood. They built informal churches, usually without crosses, so she needn't worry. The Church hierarchy was de-emphasized.

Superwasp explained all this to Kitty, assuring her that Congregational Churches today did not have crosses and were not at all threatening. In fact, they were almost not churches at all! But when we reached the church and opened the vestibule door, a huge cross, embedded on a very visible bulletin board, greeted them. "What is this?" questioned Kitty. "I thought you said there were no crosses!" My husband, as perplexed as my mother, said, "Oh don't pay any attention to that, Kitty, it's just a bulletin board. It's not part of the Church itself." They then passed through the vestibule into the Church and there, on the altar, was *another* huge cross. My husband was speechless, but Kitty was not. "Oy Vey," she exclaimed, "I'm going to church!"

MISSING KITTY

Maybe the relationship between Jewish mothers and daughters is always complicated, I really don't know since I only had one. But I am a Jewish mother and have been blessed with having a wonderful relationship with my daughter who is also my best friend.

Kitty, however, was a different story—although my daughter always said that once my mother was gone I would end up missing her a lot because she was such a big part of my life. This was absolutely true; she couldn't have been more right!

Kitty was fairly immobile for the last fifteen years of her life. She had had a back operation when she was in her late seventies, but she hadn't done much rehab and, in the decades prior to her death, she was in a lot of pain. She adjusted to this by ordering a big leather chair for her library in New York and having it placed right next to the telephone where she could wait for phone calls from kids, grandkids and great grand-kids—always a source of contention when they, especially the boys, didn't call often enough.

One day, when I went over to see Kitty she acted quite cold toward me, which was always her way of saying she was mad at me. After several attempts at normal conversation, I asked her, "What was wrong? Why was she angry?" "I'm mad at your son," she said heaving one of her regular big sighs. "What in the world did he do?" I inquired, searching my brain for what he could have possibly done to make her so mad. At this point he had graduated from Yale and was living in London, so his main contact with Kitty was through telephone calls. "Well," she said, with pursed lips and a huge frown. "He didn't call me on *his* birthday."

During those years, instead of one or two good housekeepers or nurses, Kitty chose to have six different part-time maids. I'm not sure they ever did much—and they cost a fortune. But having lots of maids made her happy, even though she complained about most of them. Her secretary would come one day a week and was her confidante in all matters; she supervised the maids, if you could call it that, and paid them and all the bills.

I tried to visit Kitty as much as possible, and bring along my grandchildren since she adored them. They loved her even though she was old; she always kept a cabinet full of toys that they could play with when they visited.

Kitty's mind was razor sharp until about two weeks before she died at the age of ninety-four. I was in the country on a Sunday when one of her housekeepers called in a panic, reporting that Kitty was babbling incoherently. My husband and I rushed down to the city and I immediately went over to her apartment, only to find that the maids had already called for an ambulance. When I arrived the medics were carrying her on a stretcher out of her building. I got into the ambulance and accompanied her to Lenox Hill Hospital's emergency room.

The ER staff settled her in a little alcove and started tests, but the attendant said I looked a little pale, was I alright? I answered that I had had a slight anxiety attack that morning, but was fine now. They then rushed me into a different little alcove across the room, strapped me into a hospital bed and put all kinds of tubes into me to start testing for problems. Obviously my blood pressure had shot up as a result of all the stress. So when my husband and daughter got to the hospital, there I was, strapped down in a hospital bed with lots of tubes inserted in different parts of my body.

I was beside myself. I kept telling them that my mother was probably dying on the other side of the room. My daughter raced back and forth between my mother and myself. Finally, my mother's doctor showed up and told them there was nothing wrong with me and to let me loose.

Kitty was in intensive care for a few days until they figured out that she had had a stroke and sent her home with a nurse. She couldn't talk and just looked up at me with big sad eyes; I'm certain that she knew she was not going to make it.

Toward the very end of her parents' lives, I remember my mother spending hours at their bedsides, holding their hands and staring at them. Morris and Esther died within months of each other, an almost insurmountable loss for Kitty who had been emotionally dependent on both of them. And now, as one generation gives to the next, it seemed to be my turn as I sat next to her, watching her.

A week after Kitty got out of the hospital, she was sitting up in her bed, turning her hands over and over and examining her finger nails—which had always been so important to her—when she died. It was a scene I will never get out of my head for the rest of my life.

Finding myself thinking about Kitty, I am amazed how my mother came across to her friends and acquaintances—adorable with her freckle-face and great figure, full of life, and the perfect company; she clearly was a lot of fun. Over the years I've frequently wished that I could have been Kitty's friend instead of her daughter; I wish I had seen her as her friends saw her—Kitty was indeed an alpha girl in her own right.

At first I couldn't imagine life without Kitty. Waves of grief would come over me in those first few weeks and months. She had always been there and I spoke to her almost every day, whether she was in a bad mood or not. She was still critical of me to her dying day, but I began to sense that she also truly loved me—it's hard to know since she was never affectionate. After she died, anytime anything important happened to me or to the kids I would rush to the phone to call her, only to realize that she wasn't there.

Going to her apartment to clean out everything and itemize her possessions so they could be divided between my brother and me was horrible, and I couldn't bear to look in her closets. Memories of my childhood kept flooding back: Blueboy, Fraulein, Katie the Cook and the myriad of other maids, Irving rushing off to golf. Also, my best friend Mary coming over in the afternoons to study with me, and Kitty coming in to ask us if we wanted anything to eat. Sitting in the library, watching Ed Sullivan with both my parents, and being sick in bed with Kitty looking so worried. Bringing the grandchildren over to play, the leather chair and the telephone.

In 2000, the Dorset Hotel, my first home in Manhattan that Kitty loved, was demolished to make room for an expansion of the Museum of Modern Art. I went over to 54th Street while it was under the wrecking ball and stood there for about an hour, tears streaming down my face. So many wonderful memories being turned to dust in a matter of minutes.

And I am crying now as I write these words. Maybe life with Kitty wasn't so bad; maybe she was just a typical Jewish mother of that generation. What I did know is that she always wanted the best for me and she saw to it that I got it. More than anyone else in the world she realized my potential and she made sure I had all the resources in the world to achieve it. And, in her own way, she loved me. I was the center of her life.

WHAT IT ALL MEANS

Now that I am in my seventies, reflecting on my father and mother, and my mother's family, I can see there is a huge difference between the culture of my generation and that of my parents, who felt very comfortable with their group of Jewish friends, Jewish country clubs, etc. Perhaps because I was quickly assimilated into Gentile schools and clubs—not to mention marriage, I never felt the need to have a social life filled with only those who shared my background. I know I'm not alone; the myriad Jewish friends my husband and I have most assuredly feel the same way.

So, after all, maybe it was because my parents and grandparents in their day were still close enough to the pogroms and the Holocaust that they sought 'safety in numbers' and were more secure socializing with their own kind. Whatever their reasons, those close friendships, the camaraderie of the Gang, wrapped my family in a world full of love and warmth that from the distance of today makes me nostalgic.

Every now and then I deeply regret the loss of the Jewish culture by my kids and grandchildren. However, I realize that you make your own choices and you can't change what has happened in your life. I look back and cherish the memories of my Jewish family and my childhood, which may never be replicated again in quite the same way.

And, as Kitty always said, *That is that*!

APPENDIX A

YIDDISH GLOSSARY

Yiddish words were a part of our upbringing and seemed particularly to come to life at holiday dinners. Kitty used most of them. Here are some of my favorites:

Alter kocker	An old man or woman or someone who acts like an old man or woman, misused by Kitty and Mimi to mean a jerk
Bubelah	Endearing term for someone you love, used by Esther in addressing me
Draikop	Scatterbrain, used a lot by Kitty and Mimi about almost everybody, especially their maids
Drek	Human feces or manure, insincere talk or flattery, again a favorite of Kitty and Mimi
Farblondzhet	Lost or bewildered or confused, used to describe people Kitty and Mimi didn't like
Fardrai zich dem kopf	Go drive yourself crazy, used by Kitty when she was annoyed by something I did

Gai avek	Go away, very popular expression in my family to get rid of unwanted children
Gai feifen ahfen yam	Go peddle your fish elsewhere (even better than *gai avek*)
Gai shlog dein kup en vant	The best! Go bang your head against a wall
Gelt	Money, used in describing Very Important People
Got in himmel	God in heaven said in despair or frustration; a favorite expression of Morris
Goyim	The non-Jewish enemy
Hak mir nit in kop	Stop banging on my head, in other words leave me alone, used by everyone in the family
Nebbish	A jerk, used to describe almost everyone in the world, except family and the Gang; also implies someone who is timid
Schlemiel	A stupid, awkward or unlucky person, used many times by everyone in the family to describe people they did not respect

Schmendrick	A stupid and ineffectual nobody, used in many conversations about maids, Gentiles and anyone who wasn't a Very Important Person
Stik drek	Manure-head
Vai iz mir	Woe is me, accompanied by heaves and sighs
Verklempt	Extremely emotional like me, according to Kitty

APPENDIX B

KITTYISMS

Kitty had a number of regular verbal and facial expressions and daily suggestions, which defined her state of mind or reaction to something said in her presence. Here are just some of them:

Cheap: This usually referred to Jews who were not refined enough, such as some of my friends at my beloved elementary school.

Crossed fingers: Also good luck used any time a wish was made.

Dirty looks: Kitty was famous for incredibly scary, withering, dirty looks when someone was misbehaving, sometimes me. Her eyes would pierce into mine and her forehead would wrinkle with disapproval (pre-Botox days). Her lips would clench together in a straight line. All together it was horrible.

Don't frown: Kitty couldn't stand it when I knitted my brows in a terrible frown, which occurred for most of my high school years and was bound to result in terrible forehead wrinkles.

For cryin' out loud: A response to something scandalous or very funny.

Get your fingers off the walls: There were two things that were necessary if you were in Kitty's home. First, no shoes in the apartment, that was a given. Second, if you needed to lean on the wall to fix your shoe or hiccup, or if you didn't use the door handle on entering the room Kitty would get very upset and shout, "Fingers off the walls!"

House guests: "After five days they stink like fish."

Real society: The group of Society Figures who made up the social elite of New York City.

She has class: The opposite of Cheap.

Society figure: Someone who has achieved the apex of social position, such as a person on Mrs. Astor's 400 list. Once, when the *New York Times* referred to me as such a creature, Kitty was overwhelmed with happiness and got on the phone for three hours.

Tsch-tsch: Wishing you good luck after spitting first.

That is that!: That is that!

Uh-huhs: If you said something that Kitty didn't like or didn't agree with she would respond with a loud "uh huh." Here are some examples:

"Mom I called Ruthie (my old friend from elementary school who was Cheap) and we are going to have a date." – "Uh-huh."

"Mom I am dating this boy I met in Europe" – "Uh-huh."

"Mom it's really not cold out, I am just going to wear a sweater" – "Uh-huh."

"Mom I can't go to see Esther and Morris today because I have to study for a test" – "Uh-huh."

"Mom I can't come out in my party dress tonight to meet your friends because it is too tight" – "Uh-huh."

"Mom my stomach is so sick I can't go to Sunday School" – "UH-HUH!"

And so on.

Very Important People: This referred to women on the society pages, friends of Morris who came to his July 4th party in the country, very rich people, Jewish philanthropists and eventually, thank God, my husband.

Weather reports: Called in to me each morning, particularly when my children were young, followed by clothing suggestions, which were always too heavy and too warm.

Here were some things that kept you in Kitty's favor:

Being polite to Kitty's relatives, friends, and employees of Madison Avenue stores and beauty salons. This is self-explanatory.

Friends with Class – see above.

Never complaining while shopping.

Smoking – If you watched "Mad Men" you will remember the popularity of smoking, not only as a habit, but as a necessary feature in one's social life in the '60s. Kitty, well aware of this, was anxious for me to smoke and hold the cigarette in the right way. Thus, began my smoking lessons in which Kitty would pose with the cigarette between her second and third fingers, turned slightly upward as it made its way to her mouth and slightly downward as it left her mouth. This was accompanied with slanting eyelids and pursed lips. Kitty as an actress was wonderful!

Very good marks – Since I was always a terrific student I didn't have to fear the wrath of Kitty if I didn't get good marks. In fact, she used to worry that I was studying too hard and would get an ulcer—the prevalent Jewish ailment at that time. I guess I enjoyed my studies, but I was also aware that life would be very uncomfortable if I failed in school.

Here is what I wasn't allowed to do:

Be rude to Mimi or Katie the Cook.

Hang my head when I met people.

Not clean my plate. If I left even one broccoli leaf on my plate, I would hear about starving Armenians and how selfish it was not to eat when I was so lucky to have food.

Say "yeah" instead of "yes." This was a crime.

Love Fraulein too much. This was something that was hard not to do in front of Kitty, but I restrained myself.

Splash Peter in the swimming pool, even though he always started it.

Steal Peter's trucks and guns at Christmas and replace them with my dolls. This was a definite no, no, because it made Mimi crazy.

Take Blueboy out of the cage if he wasn't already out when Kitty entered the room.